Muslim–Christian enco

D0194415

Relations between Muslims and Christians have become strained in the wake of the Rushdie affair. That affair brought out aspects of Muslim resentment against the West which had been smouldering beneath the surface, and also strengthened negative views of Islam among many Christians.

William Montgomery Watt, one of the leading authorities on Islam in the West, shows that throughout history Muslim–Christian encounters have been beset by myths and misperceptions, many of which endure to the present day. He describes how the myths originated, how they developed, and how they continue to blight Muslim and Christian perceptions of each other. Arguing that both Muslims and Christians need to have a more accurate knowledge and a more positive appreciation of the other religion, Professor Montgomery Watt looks forward to fruitful cooperation on the world scene between Muslims, Christians and members of other religions, and suggests how this might be achieved.

The outcome of over fifty years of study, reflection and writing on Islam and Christianity, *Muslim–Christian Encounters* will be of particular interest to students of Islam, religion, history and sociology.

William Montgomery Watt is Emeritus Professor in Arabic and Islamic Studies at the University of Edinburgh. He is the author of many books on Islam and the West, most recently *Islamic Fundamentalism and Modernity* and *Islam and Christianity Today*.

Muslim–Christian encounters

Perceptions and misperceptions

William Montgomery Watt

ROUTLEDGE

London and New York

First published 1991
by Routledge
11 New Fetter Lane, London EC4P 4EE

Simultaneously published in the USA and Canada
by Routledge
a division of Routledge, Chapman and Hall Inc.
29 West 35th Street, New York, NY 10001

© 1991 William Montgomery Watt

Typeset in Baskerville by
Pat and Anne Murphy, Highcliffe-on-Sea, Dorset
Printed and bound in Great Britain by
Biddles Ltd, Guildford and King's Lynn

All rights reserved. No part of this book may be reprinted or reproduced or utilized in any form or by any electronic, mechanical, or other means, now known or hereafter invented, including photocopying and recording, or in any information storage or retrieval system, without permission in writing from the publishers.

British Library Cataloguing in Publication Data
Watt, W. Montgomery (William Montgomery) *1909*–
Muslim–Christian encounters.
1. Christianity. Relations with Islam. 2. Islam. Relations with Christianity
I. Title
261.27

Library of Congress Cataloging in Publication Data
Watt, W. Montgomery (William Montgomery)
Muslim–Christian encounters:perceptions and misperceptions/by William Montgomery Watt.
p. cm.
Includes bibliographical references and index.
1. Islam–Relations–Christianity. 2. Christianity and other religions–Islam. I. Title.
BP172.W33 1991 90–45261
CIP

ISBN 0–415–05410–9
0–415–05411–7 (pbk)

Contents

Chapter 1

The Christianity encountered by Islam

When one begins to think about the Christianity encountered by Muḥammad and the first Muslims, it has to be realized that it was very different from the Christianity we know today. Round about AD 600 there was a main body of Christians constituting the Great Church, which later divided into the Roman Catholic, Eastern Orthodox and Protestant churches of today; but there were also important bodies of Christians who had been expelled from the Great Church as heretics, notably those often known as the Monophysites (Jacobites and Copts) and the Nestorians. Most of the Christians of Egypt, Palestine, Syria and Iraq – the lands first occupied by the Muslims – probably belonged to these heretical bodies. To these bodies also belonged most of the Christians in Arabia itself.

VARIOUS CULTURAL DIFFERENCES

The religious distinction between orthodoxy and heresy was closely linked with ethnic or perhaps rather cultural differences. The Great Church was intimately associated with the ruling groups in the Byzantine or Eastern Roman Empire, and these were essentially Greek in culture. The Monophysite heresy, on the other hand, had become the focus of anti-Greek feeling both among the Copts or native Egyptians and among the Jacobites of Syria, who are sometimes described as West Syrians. The Nestorian heresy had played a similar role for those often called East Syrians, and their opposition to the Greeks was such that they had been expelled from the Byzantine Empire and by the year 600 had established their main centre in Iraq in the Sassanian (Persian) Empire. The Great Church also included the Christians of western Europe, whose culture was basically Latin and who in 600 were divided among various Frankish and other petty kingdoms; but in the early seventh century the Arabs were not in contact with these.

In the ecumenical councils of the Church (such as those of Nicaea in 325 and of Chalcedon in 451) the bishops of Greek culture had played a dominant role, and the formulations of trinitarian and christological doctrine officially accepted by the councils were largely in terms of the type of Greek philosophy then current in the Byzantine Empire. The bishops of Latin culture were in general less philosophically minded than the Greeks but acquiesced in the Greek formulations. It is perhaps worth noting, however, that the Latin terms for trinitarian doctrine (one *substantia*, three *personae*) were accepted as equivalent to the Greek (one *ousia*, three *hypostaseis*) although they are not identical, since *substantia* corresponds etymologically to *hypostasis*. The bishops representing the Egyptians and the East and West Syrians rejected the Greek formulations and adopted various alternatives, with the result that they were excluded from the Great Church and in the case of the Nestorians from the Christian empire.

Most people of today, when they look at the detailed doctrinal discussions about the Trinity and the person of Christ, have the impression of being in a labyrinth of abstractions, whose relevance to actual Christian living is hard to discern. I hold that one can begin to make a little sense of the discussions if one asks *why* the protagonists argued as they did, and tries to answer this question by looking at features of their cultural background. What did they consider to be the chief problem of human life, and how did they understand Jesus to have solved this? In other words, what are the fundamental beliefs underlying the arguments, and how are these related to cultural differences?

ORTHODOXY

Greek culture was, of course, far from being homogeneous, since under its umbrella had come people from various backgrounds where the native languages, such as the speech of Lycaonia,[1] had not achieved the status of literary languages, as had Coptic and Syriac. One feature of Greek culture was its belief in orthodoxy.[2] It is not fortuitous that the eastern section of the Great Church has come to be known as the Orthodox Church, for it was here that complete agreement in belief was held to be the basis for the unity of the community of Christians. The western section, on the other hand, was more concerned with the catholicity of the church, that is, the unity of the church throughout the world, and this was to be maintained by recognition of the authority of the hierarchy derived from the original apostles. The orthodox vision of a community homogeneous in belief and united in worship was important for the church as a whole; but in practice the vision could be perverted into the tool of a dominant majority tyrannizing over minorities. Orthodoxy was taken to mean the acceptance of credal formulations, and these were the subject of negotiation between different parties at the ecumenical councils. In these negotiations minorities like the Egyptians and Syrians lost out, and had to choose between abandoning some of their inmost convictions and leaving the Great Church.

Greek culture in pre-Christian times had been characterized by a dualistic conception of the human person, in which the soul was regarded as the real person and the body as a mere instrument. There had even been a tradition in Greek thought according to which the body (*sōma*) was the tomb (*sēma*) of the soul, so that real life only began when the soul was freed from the body. An early Christian thinker of Greek outlook was Clement of Alexandria (d. 215?) who was clearly not Egyptian despite spending much of his life in Egypt, and who aimed at a defence of the Christian faith in terms of the current philosophy. For him the rational soul was the essential person, but people have become irrational in thought and conduct, in that sin consists in the conquest of reason by sensual pleasure. This being the main problem for humanity, the unique work of Christ was seen as the bringing of true knowledge and the freeing of reason from the bonds of irrational nature. True knowledge is held to lead to right action, and the ideal human life is one in which rationality is developed to the fullest extent.

A later stage in Greek thinking can be seen in the work of Gregory of Nyssa (d. *c.*395), who was one of those mainly responsible for the trinitarian doctrine of the Council of Constantinople (381) that Christ is of the same being (*homoousios*) as the Father, not of similar being (*homoiousios*). Gregory emphasized that in Christ we see operations identical with those of the Father, e.g. giving life and health, cleansing and guiding. The human person for Gregory is essentially the soul, created at the same time as its body. The body is not in itself evil, but through its connection with the body the soul becomes stained with sensual passions and affections, and the work of Christ is to cleanse the soul from these. At the resurrection the soul is given a new imperishable and impassible body.

These brief statements are perhaps sufficient to give an idea of the

Greek culture on which the credal formulations of the Great Church were based.

THE MONOPHYSITES

The difference between Greek culture and that of the Egyptian and Syrian Christians is most clearly seen by looking at the Christianity which developed into the Coptic church. Among the well-known features of pre-Christian Egypt are the practice of mummification and the building of pyramids. These show an intense interest in overcoming human mortality, and the same interest is to be found in many Christian writers of native Egyptian origin, notably Athanasius (d. 373). In such writers we find a monistic conception of the human person; that is, though the person consists of soul and body, the body is as much part of the person as the soul. According to Athanasius human beings are by nature perishable or mortal like animals, but by the gift of reason (not here identified with the soul) God made them immortal. Human beings lost this immortality, however, because they were deceived by the devil, who, and not the body, is regarded as the source of evil. The work of Christ according to Athanasius is twofold. On the one hand, he accepts the penalty of death on behalf of sinful humanity. More important, however, is the incarnation of the divine Word in Jesus by which his human nature becomes incorruptible and is resurrected after death. Jesus really died, since that was necessary to achieve salvation for humanity; but, because his body was united to the Word, it was no longer subject to corruption, so that on the third day the resurrection took place. Through association with the body of Christ Christians share in this incorruptibility or immortality. Athanasius has a sentence which sums up his teaching: "Christ becomes incarnate that he may make us divine." It is difficult not to see in this line of thought a Christianizing of the ancient Egyptian preoccupation with death and the escape from it.

From this account of the teaching of Athanasius it is possible to see how it was inevitable for later Egyptian or Coptic thinkers to adopt Monophysitism, the doctrine that there is a single divine–human nature in Christ. The central problem of human life, the problem of mortality, was solved by the union of the divine Word with human nature, in such a way that human nature became incorruptible. On the other hand, if in Christ the divine and human natures remained distinct, as the Greeks maintained, then human nature had not become incorruptible, and the human nature of ordinary Christians remained subject to death. To those in the Egyptian tradition this was tantamount to a denial of the saving work of Christ.

The other branch of the Monophysites, the Jacobites, or West Syrians, held the doctrine of the one divine–human nature for a slightly different reason. Their views can conveniently be studied in the writings of Severus of Antioch (d. 538), who was Patriarch of Antioch from 512 to 518. Severus holds a monistic view of the human person, at least to the extent that he does not regard salvation as becoming free from the body. For Severus, as for many Semites, the great problem for human beings is the attainment of security in respect of the economic and material side of life. Suffering and hardship were in general regarded as punishment for sin, though in some cases they were used by God to recall his servants to a better life. In the thought of Severus God is primarily "power in action" (*energeia*), not reason; and the incarnation of the divine Word in Jesus means that in him we see a divine–human or theandric *energeia*. By this theandric *energeia* human beings were delivered from the demonic powers which enticed them to sin and incur the penalties of sin; and Christians may obtain the benefits of this deliverance by participating in the Eucharist. Central in the thought of Severus is this conception of the divine power manifesting itself in and through a human life, and so bringing security to humanity as a whole. This result could not be achieved, however, if the divine and human natures in Jesus remained separate. This latter view, that Jesus is both divine and human, but that the two natures are distinct is, of course, the official view of the ecumenical councils and of most Christians today, and is known as Dyophysitism.

THE NESTORIANS

When we turn to the East Syrians or Nestorians, we find that a central point in their thinking was that God is eternal and impassible. It was for this reason that they objected to the term *theotokos* or "God-bearer" applied to Mary, since God the eternal cannot be a human infant. Nestorius and his followers emphasized the humanity of Jesus because it was in his humanity that he won a victory over Satan, by "humbling himself and taking the form of a servant".[3] He was tempted as human beings are, but he did not yield to the temptations; and in this struggle he had no advantages which we may not also have. Nestorius seems to be suggesting that previously people could not detect the deceptions of Satan and did not believe that it was possible for humanity to fulfil the commandments perfectly, and thus they acquiesced in disobedience; but now they know that obedience is possible for human nature and so have become capable of obedience. Both for Christ's humanity and for us the assistance of divine grace is not excluded. It was in his humanity that Christ overcame Satan, but in his self-emptying to take the form of a servant there was for humanity a supreme model of humility. Nestorius, however, had great difficulty in explaining how God's eternity and impassibility can be united with temporal humanity, since God cannot suffer. He placed some emphasis on unity of will, since God's will can operate in temporal circumstances, but this unity of will was a consequence of the unity of humanity and divinity and not its ground.

KNOWLEDGE OF CHRISTIANITY IN MECCA

Of the Christians of Muḥammad's time the Nestorians and the Monophysites were the most important cultural groups distinct from those lumped together under the heading of "Greek" culture. Recently the theologian Hans Küng has taken up a line of thought followed by earlier German scholars and has suggested that the form of Christianity best known to the people of Mecca at that time was that of small groups of Christians from a Jewish background, who had never accepted the credal formulations of the Great Church, but had managed to maintain their existence in relative isolation. Such groups would accept Jesus as Messiah but not as a divine hypostasis.[4] It is impossible to know to what extent these Jewish Christians or the more numerous Arab Monophysites and Nestorians influenced the ideas about Christianity current in Mecca. In some ways the general cultural outlook of the Meccan Arabs seems to be closest to that of the Nestorians. Moreover, despite the presence of numerous groups of Christians among both nomadic and settled Arabs, there can have been very few persons with a scholarly knowledge of Christianity, and these would be some clerics and monks.[5] The ordinary Christian Arab had presumably only a meagre knowledge of his religion.

There was no Arabic translation of the Bible or even of the New Testament, though there may have been translations of short passages in monasteries and similar places.[6] The statement of Ibn-Isḥāq[7] that Waraqa ibn-Nawfal, the cousin of Muḥammad's wife Khadīja, was a Christian and knew the books, could only mean that he had read some of the Bible in Syriac or had had it read to him. A number of Meccan merchants, including Muḥammad, had travelled to Gaza and Damascus in the Byzantine Empire, and some to Christian Abyssinia; but such persons would generally learn only about the external features of Christianity unless they were specially interested. There were also some Byzantine Christians in Mecca from time to time, perhaps chiefly craftsmen. Something was known about Judaism in Mecca from the presence of Jewish clans in Medina and in various Arabian oases. Thus people in Mecca knew of the existence of the Jewish and Christian religions, but had little accurate information about them.

CHRISTIAN WEAKNESSES

For a due appreciation of the first encounter between Islam and Christianity it is necessary for Christians to be aware of the weaknesses of the Christianity of that period. There are three main points.

In the first place Orthodox Christianity, that is, the Great Church in general, was too closely associated with the Byzantine Empire after it became the official religion of the Empire in the reign of Constantine. Had the Meccans become Christians, they would inevitably have become in some respects subject to the Byzantines. For the sake of their trading interests, however, it was important for them to maintain neutrality between the Byzantine and Sassanian Empires. About 590 or a little later a Meccan called ʻUthmān ibn al-Ḥuwayrith, who had become a Christian, apparently tried to get the Meccans to accept him as a kind of prince by saying he could get special privileges for them from the Byzantines; and it may well have been the religious aspect as well as his pretensions to lordship which made them reject his proposal.[8]

In the second place, official Greek theology as defined by the ecumenical councils had become much too abstract and was completely beyond the grasp of the ordinary Christian. The Monophysites and Nestorians, in defending their positions against the official formulations, had also become somewhat abstract. This meant that any Christians whom the Meccans were likely to meet would be incapable of explaining the subtleties of Christian doctrine. It is not surprising that inadequate and erroneous ideas about Christianity were current in Mecca, but this is something for which Christians themselves were responsible.

Last, the rejection of the Copts, Jacobites and Nestorians by the Great Church was almost certainly a factor facilitating the conversion to Islam of members of these groups. Essentially the decision of the

Great Church that these were heretics was a failure to make due provision for cultural diversity among Christians. Christians today should be thinking seriously about the fact that in its homelands their religion has virtually been replaced by Islam, and should be asking whether God has brought this about because of Christian failures.

Chapter 2

The Qur'ānic perception of Christianity

THE GENERAL CONCEPTION OF PROPHETHOOD

The Qur'ānic perception of other religions in general and of Judaism and Christianity in particular is inevitably dependent on the level of historical understanding current in Mecca and the rest of Arabia about AD 600; and this level was distinctly low. The Arabs had no written historical documents. There were some inscriptions from earlier kingdoms, but it is doubtful if any could read them, still less appreciate their significance. Thus for the Arabs, history depended on oral tradition. They knew something of the history of their own tribes and clans for a few generations back; but the history of Arab tribes was mostly a history of how tribes grew in power through one or more outstanding leaders, continued to be strong for a generation or two, then faded back into unimportance. A sense of the transience of human communities was probably strengthened by the observation of sites which had once been inhabited but were no longer so. In a number of Qur'ānic passages the Muslims are told to travel through the land and see the disasters that had come upon the former inhabitants because they had not heeded the words of their prophet.[1] The merchants of Mecca had visited the Byzantine, Sassanian and Abyssinian Empires, but they probably had no idea of the length of time for which these had existed. Arabs thought in terms of human generations, not in terms of decades or centuries. It was thus impossible for them to conceive of a community like the Jewish community with a continuous history lasting well over a thousand years, some thirty or forty generations.

A further feature of the Arab historical outlook was the belief in the unchangingness of the conditions of human life and society, and a consequent abhorrence of all novelty. One of the complaints against Muḥammad by the pagans of Mecca was that prophethood was unknown in Arabia, and in the Qur'ān Muḥammad was told to insist explicitly that his prophethood was not something novel (46:9). The stories of former prophets, which are reckoned to constitute about a quarter of the Qur'ān, are thus not merely encouragement for Muḥammad and his followers but also an assertion that he had a long spiritual ancestry and that previous prophets had had similar experiences to his. A common form of the story tells how, after the prophet has called on his people to believe in God and to worship and serve God alone, they have rejected his message and then been struck down by disaster. In suras 7, 11 and 26 there are parallel accounts of Noah, Lot and three Arabian prophets, Hūd, Ṣāliḥ and Shu'ayb, and there are shorter references to these elsewhere; sometimes Abraham, Moses and others are added.[2] In Sura 7:59–64 the account of Noah begins and ends thus:

> Noah we sent to his people, saying, O my people,
> serve God; apart from him you have no god.
> I fear for you (otherwise) the punishment of a great day.
> Said the council of his people,
> We see you in clear error. . . .
> Yet they disbelieved him;
> and him and those with him we saved in the ark;
> but drowned those disbelieving in our signs,
> a blind people they.

The Arabian prophets make similar appeals to their people to believe in God and serve him alone, but the punishments are different. Lot accuses his people of sexual immorality; but again disaster befalls them while he is rescued.

In the present context an important point to notice is that normally a prophet is sent to preach monotheism to his own people, and that they are assumed to be worshippers of many gods or none. The following verse (23:44) may indicate how Muslims felt about prophethood while they were still more conscious of the opposition to Muḥammad than of his success:

> Then we sent our messengers one after other.
> When to a community its messenger came,
> they counted him false;
> so we caused them to follow one the other (to disaster).

Mostly a prophet seems to have been one who gathered round himself a community of first-generation believers. There was no suggestion that a prophet might go to a community of believers in God in order to bring them some further knowledge about him. Men such as the book-prophets of the Old Testament were unthinkable, and it is perhaps significant that none of them is named in the Qur'ān apart from Jonah; but Jonah is not an exception, since it is now held by Christian scholars that the book of that name, despite its spiritual profundity, was not written by an actual person called Jonah.

It is implied in the Qur'ān that all prophets teach the same message in essentials, especially the belief that there is no god but God, and that on the Last Day everyone will be brought before God to be judged. The following passage (3:81, 85) describes something which presumably happened before creation:

God took the covenant of the prophets,
What I have given you of Book and wisdom –
when a messenger comes to you confirming what you have,
you must believe in him and support him. He said,
Do you assent and accept my task on that (condition)?
They said, We assent . . .
He who seeks other than *islām* as religion,
it will not be accepted from him.

In the phrase at the end of this quotation the word *islām* appears to have its general sense of "submission (to God)", and thus to be a description of the religion proclaimed by all the prophets, not solely that proclaimed by Muḥammad. In a similar way the word *muslim* or "one submitting" is sometimes used for an adherent of this general religion. The word "messenger" or "apostle" (*rasūl*), when used in a technical sense, means virtually the same as "prophet" (*nabī*), namely, one who conveys to his own people a message (*risāla*) from God. The commonest title for Muḥammad in Arabic is Messenger of God, and because of this it tends to connote the developed conception of prophethood, as it was in Muḥammad's last years when he had become leader and head of the community; but this connotation should not be read into the earlier Qur'ānic usages.

This covenant of the prophets seems to follow on from a primordial covenant between God and the human race as a whole (7:172f.):

One time your Lord from the loins of the sons of Adam
took their posterity
and made them testify about themselves,
Am not I your Lord?
They said, Yes, we testify –

lest you should say on the Day of Resurrection,
Of this we have been unaware;
or should say, Our fathers before gave partners (to God)
and we were a posterity after them;
will you destroy us for what the falsifiers did?

It would probably be going too far to hold that this implied that all human beings had an innate knowledge of God, but it does imply that all have a capacity for responding to a prophet. The point is mentioned here since it is part of the background of the religious history of the human race as portrayed in the Qur'ān.

THE PERCEPTION OF JUDAISM

Since this was the conception of prophethood and of the history of prophets held by the early Muslims, it was impossible for them to have any adequate idea of the history of Judaism and Christianity. It is also important to realize how much is *not* said in the Qur'ān, since the modern western reader with some knowledge of these religions has a framework into which he fits the details given in isolation from one another in the Qur'ān. Thus there are stories about Noah, Abraham and Moses (all regarded as prophets) and other Old Testament characters, but virtually no indication is given of how they relate to one another in time. Similarly there are many details about Moses from his infancy onwards, but events are treated in isolation and not put into chronological order.

There was some idea that there had been a series of prophets in the Israelite community. This community was spoken of as the Banū Isrā'īl (sons of Israel) in much the same way as Arab tribes were often spoken of as Banū N (sons of N); but it was also regarded as having been based originally on the scripture given to Moses as a prophet. Thus it is stated:[3]

We gave Moses the Book
and caused messengers to follow him.

The continuity of the Banū Isrā'īl as a tribe is perhaps indicated by the assertion that:[4]

We bestowed on him (Abraham) Isaac and Jacob,
and we appointed the prophethood and the Book
to be among his posterity.

On the other hand, when Muḥammad found himself rejected as a prophet by the Jews of Medina, the Qur'ān says (2:130–4) that, after Abraham had charged his sons and Jacob to submit (as *muslims*) to the Lord of the worlds, and Jacob had similarly charged his sons and they had accepted,

> that is a community which has passed away.

It is further to be noted that there is nothing in the Qur'ān about Joshua and the settlement of the Banū Isrā'īl in the Promised Land, nothing about the establishment of the kingdom under David, nothing about the Exile and the return from exile. There is a passage (17:4–7) about a warning given to the Banū Isrā'īl of two punishments, and one could be the Exile; but this is not made explicit. David is spoken of in the Qur'ān as a prophet who received a scripture called the Zabūr, which is taken to be the Psalms (4:163; 17:55). The mountains and birds are said to have been made to join him in praising God; and this could be a reference to passages in the Psalms calling on creatures to praise the Lord.[5] Both David and Solomon were given jurisdiction (21:78–80), which suggests that they were rulers; and it is also stated that David's kingship was made strong (38:20). He is likewise said to have been shown how to make coats of mail (34:10f.; 38:17–20). All this, however, fails to give any idea of David's significance in the history of the Israelites.

Moses is spoken of as a prophet who received from God a book or scripture called the *tawrāt* (6:154; cf.5:44). While this word may be identified with the Torah, what is said about it in the Qur'ān would not give Muslims any idea of the character of the Pentateuch, still less of the Old Testament as a whole, since the *tawrāt* seems to have consisted largely of legal rules. It is nowhere suggested that the historical material about Noah, the patriarchs, the early life of Moses and the Exodus comes from the *tawrāt*. There is, of course, in the Qur'ān historical material about various events in ancient history, but, rather than give people fresh information about things unknown to them, it seems instead to be drawing lessons from events about which they already know something. For this purpose a brief description or reference is sufficient, as may be seen by comparing the passage about Noah just quoted with the Biblical accounts.

It is not made clear why there was a need for later prophets. It may be because the Israelites relapsed into unbelief amounting almost to paganism:

God made a covenant with the Banū Isrā'īl . . .
and God said, I am with you;
if you observe the Worship and pay the Alms,
and believe my messengers and support them,
and give God a good loan, I shall remit your sins,
and bring you to Gardens through which rivers flow.
Whoever of you disbelieves after that
has erred from the way.
So for their breaking their covenant
we have cursed them and hardened their heart.
(5.12f.)

A more positive statement is the following:

We sent down the Torah in which is guidance and light;
by it the prophets who submitted (to God – *aslamū*)
gave judgement for the Jews
according to that (part) of the Book of God
they were entrusted with and were witnesses for.
(5:44)

There are also some obscure references to misdemeanours of the Jews in 7:167–9.

After he went to Medina Muḥammad was in contact with the Jewish groups there, and the Qur'ān not surprisingly gives some of the arguments to be used against them, especially against their claim that they alone had a true knowledge of God. The main apologetic argument came to be that the Qur'ān presented the pure religion of Abraham, who was a *ḥanīf*, a *muslim* (in the general sense), and neither a Jew nor a Christian.[6] This last statement is strictly speaking true, despite the fact that Jews and Christians reverence Abraham as a kind of ancestor of their religions, and it proves that there is a true knowledge of God apart from these religions. Such arguments, however, did not help the Muslims to form any clearer idea of Judaism.

THE PERCEPTION OF CHRISTIANITY

The previous chapter tried to show how for Muḥammad and other Meccans the opportunities for learning about Christianity were limited. Many had been on trading journeys to Syria, as had Muḥammad himself, but would not have engaged much in religious discussions with Christians. The few Christians in Mecca were probably temporary foreign residents in the main. In the early passages of the Qur'ān, however, there are some very friendly references to Christians.

Those who believe and those who are Jews,
and the Christians and the Sabians,
whoever believes in God and the Last Day and acts uprightly,
they have their reward from their Lord.

(2:62)

This acceptance of Jews and Christians as fellow believers in God is in line with the assurance given by Waraqa, Khadīja's cousin, to Muḥammad that the revelations which he was receiving were comparable to those received by Moses.[7]

A revelation received by Muḥammad soon after the Hijra when he was having trouble with the Jews of Medina contrasts the Christians very favourably with them:

You (Muḥammad) will indeed find the most hostile of people
to the believers are the Jews and the idolaters.
You will indeed find the closest in love to the believers
are those who say, We are Christians.
That is because among them are priests and monks,
and they are not proud.

(5:82)

This commendation of the Christians may reflect the kindness shown earlier to a group of Muslims in the Christian Empire of Abyssinia (or Ethiopia) when they went there to avoid persecution in Mecca.

A passage which is probably from a slightly later date again speaks favourably of the Christians but criticizes their monastic tradition:

We gave Jesus the Gospel
and in the hearts of his followers set kindness and mercy,
and the monastic state; but that they invented –
we did not prescribe it for them –
(it was) only out of a desire to please God,
but they did not observe it aright.

(57:27)

The following passage seems to show an awareness of the divisions between Christians, though it could conceivably refer to disputes between Christians and Jews. The covenant could be the new covenant or testament as understood by the first Christians:

> With those who say, We are Christians,
> we made a covenant;
> but they forgot a part of the admonition.
> So we stirred up enmity and hatred among them
> until the day of resurrection.
>
> (5:14)

The next arguments between the Christians and Jews are referred to in the next passage:

> The Jews say, The Christians have no basis (for belief);
> and the Christians say, The Jews have no basis,
> though both read the Book . . .
> God will judge between them on the day of resurrection
> about that in which they have been differing.
>
> (2:113)

This appears to suggest that the claims of Jews and Christians cancel one another out.

This criticism of the Jews and Christians was mainly due to the fact that neither would admit the prophethood of Muḥammad, while each maintained that the truth was exclusively theirs, as in the following verse:

> They say, Be Jews or Christians and you will be guided.
> Say (to them), No, but the creed of Abraham as a *ḥanīf*;
> and he was not of the idolaters.
>
> (2.135)

It is then insisted that Abraham and his immediate descendants were neither Jews nor Christians,[8] the point being, as already noted, that Abraham and the others were admittedly "guided" and yet did not receive this guidance as Jews or Christians; and this implies that there must be another source of guidance. (Abraham, as in Muslim eyes a prophet, could himself receive guidance.) The word *ḥanīf* is used in the Qur'ān to denote a monotheist who is neither Jew nor Christian, and it is applied only to Abraham and to Muḥammad and his followers.[9] It is in fact part of the Qur'ānic apologetic against the older religions. Early Muslim scholars named a few men slightly prior to Muhammad whom they alleged to be *ḥanīfs*, but there is no evidence that any of these used the word of himself, even if the description applied. In pre-Islamic poetry and in Christian Arabic the word means heathen or idolater.[10]

What may be regarded as the beginning of the Christian story in the Qur'ān is some legendary material which is not found in the New Testament:

God chose Adam and Noah and the family of Abraham
and the family of 'Imrān above all people,
descendants one of other; God is Hearer, Knower.
One time the wife of 'Imrān said, My Lord,
I have vowed to you what is in my womb (as) dedicated;
accept (this) from me; you are Hearer, Knower.
When she bore her she said, My Lord, I have borne her
a female – and God well knew what she had borne;
the male is not as the female – I have named her Mary;
and I commit her and her offspring to you
(for protection) from the accursed Satan.
Her Lord accepted her graciously, and made her grow in grace.
Zechariah took charge of her.
Whenever Zechariah entered the sanctuary to her,
he found beside her a provision.
He said, O Mary, how have you this?
She said, It is from God;
God provides for whom he will generously.

(3:31–7)

'Imrān is the Arabic form given to Amram, father of Moses, Aaron and Miriam in the Bible. Some people in Mecca seem to have confused Mary with Miriam, since the name would be the same in Arabic, and so Mary is addressed as "sister of Aaron" in 19:28.

This passage continues with an account of the birth of John the Baptist which is roughly in accordance with Luke, 1:5–25, 57–64:

Then Zechariah prayed his Lord and said,
My Lord, give me from yourself a goodly offspring,
you are hearer of prayer. The angels called him
as he stood worshipping in the sanctuary,
God gives you tidings of Yaḥyā (John),
confirming a word from God, a leader,
abstinent, a prophet, (one) of the upright.
He said, How shall there be to me a boy,
now age has come upon me and my wife is barren?
He said, Thus (shall it be): God does what he will.
He said, My Lord appoint for me a sign.

He said, Your sign is that for three days
you shall not speak to the people except by gesture;
but remember your Lord much,
and give glory evening and morning.

(3:38–41)

There is a similar but longer version in 19:1–15.

The latter is followed by an account of the annunciation to Mary and the birth of Jesus ('Īsā):

Mention in the Book Mary, when she withdrew
from her people to an easterly place.
She took in front of them a curtain;
then we sent to her our Spirit,
who appeared to her as a handsome person.
She said, I take refuge with the Merciful from you,
if you fear (God).
He said, I am only the messenger of your Lord
to give you a pure boy.
She said, How shall I have a boy,
when no man touched me and I was not wanton.
He said, Thus (shall it be); your Lord said,
It is easy for me, and (it is) that we may make him
a sign for the people, and a mercy from us;
it is a thing decided. So she conceived him,
and withdrew with him to a far place,
and the birth-pangs drove her to the trunk of a palm;
she said, Would I had died before this,
and had been in oblivion, forgotten.
Then he called her from beneath her, Grieve not;
your Lord has set beneath you a stream.
Shake towards you the trunk of the palm,
and it will drop moist, ripe (dates) on you.
So eat and drink and be of good cheer;
and if you see any person, say,
I have vowed to the Merciful a fast,
and today I speak to nobody.
She brought him to her people carrying him.
They said, O Mary, You have done a thing unheard of.
O sister of Aaron, your father was not an evil man,
nor your mother wanton.

She pointed to him; they said, How shall we speak
with one in the cradle, a child?
He said, I am God's servant;
he has given me the Book and made me a prophet.
He has made me blessed wherever I am,
and has enjoined on me the Worship and Alms,
so long as I live; and (to be) dutiful to my mother;
and has not made me oppressive, impious.
Peace is on me the day I was born, the day I shall die,
and the day I shall be raised alive.
That is Jesus, son of Mary –
the statement of the truth of which there is no doubt.
(19:16–34)

While the account of the annunciation is not unlike that in Luke, 1:26–38, the story of the birth is completely different, so that it seems to Christians to be about another event. There is no mention of Mary's relationship to Joseph, nor of the journey to Bethlehem, nor of the manger. There are no obvious sources for this version of the birth, but it may well be that there were Christians in Arabia who held some such view. What is important is that according to most exegetes the Qur'ān teaches the virginal conception of Jesus, even though some modern Muslim commentators try to deny this.[11] The Qur'ān is more concerned than the gospels to defend Mary from the accusation of unchastity; and the words in the last verse quoted – "the statement of the truth" – probably imply that this passage puts an end to such slanders by explaining the precise manner of the conception. The acceptance of the virginal conception of Jesus by Muslims together with their denial of his divinity would seem to show that there is no necessary connection between virginal conception and divinity, and reflection tends to support this; but what can be said is that for those who believe in the divinity *on other grounds* there is an appropriateness in the virginal conception.

The fullest statement of the nature of the prophethood of Jesus is given in another account of the annunciation:

One time the angels said, O Mary,
God tells you of a Word from himself,
whose name is the Messiah, son of Mary,
eminent in this world and the hereafter,
one of those brought near.
He will speak to the people in his cradle.

and as a man, and one of the upright.
She said, My Lord, how shall I have a child
when no man has touched me?
He said, Thus (shall it be); God creates what he wills;
when he decides on a thing,
he only says to it, Be, and it is.
(God) will teach him the Book and the Wisdom
and the Torah and the Gospel,
and (make him) a messenger to the Banū Isrā'īl,
(saying), I have brought you a sign from your Lord;
I shall fashion for you from clay the form of a bird,
and I shall breathe into it,
so that it becomes a bird by God's permission;
and I shall heal the blind and the leper,
and bring the dead to life by God's permission,
and I shall announce to you what you may eat
and what you may store in your houses.
In that is a sign for you if you are believers.
(I come) confirming what is with me of the Torah
and making lawful for you some of what was forbidden you.
I have come to you with a sign from your Lord;
so fear God and obey me.
God is my Lord and your Lord;
so serve him; this is a straight path.
When Jesus perceived their unbelief, he said,
Who are my helpers towards God?
The disciples said, We are God's helpers;
bear witness that we are *muslimūn*.
O our Lord, we have believed in what you sent down
and followed the messenger.
Write us among the witnesses.

(3:45–53)

The name of ''Helpers'' (*Anṣār*) was given to Muḥammad's supporters in Medina, and it also has an affinity with *Naṣārā*, Christians. The word *ḥawāriyyūn* is used in the Qur'ān only for the disciples of Jesus.

The miracles mentioned in the previous passage come also in another passage though without the legal prescriptions, and then it is added:

and (remember) how I restrained the Banū Isrā'īl from you
when you came to them with the Evidences,
and the unbelievers of them said,
This is nought but magic clear.

(5:110)

In these passages it may be noticed that Jesus is sent to the Banū Isrā'īl, and thus is one of the posterity of Abraham. He is, however, regarded as a lawgiver, "confirming" the Torah, though with some variations. The miracle of the clay birds becoming alive, which is not in the New Testament, is well known to scholars from various heretical gospels.[12]

There are two points at which the Qur'ān appears to deny matters central to the belief of the vast majority of Christians. It appears to deny that Jesus died on the cross, and it rejects his divinity. For the denial of the death on the cross the basic text is:

And because of their (the Jews') unbelief
and their saying against Mary a great slander,
and for their saying, We killed the Messiah,
Jesus, son of Mary, the messenger of God –
though they did not kill him and did not crucify him,
but it was made to seem to them.
Those who differ about him are in doubt about him;
they have no knowledge about him but follow opinion.
Certainly they did not kill him,
but God raised him to himself.

(4:156–8)

Less clear is:

One time God said, O Jesus, I am completing your term
and raising you to myself,
and purifying you from the unbelievers,
and setting your followers above the unbelievers
till the day of resurrection.
Then to me is your return, and I shall judge between you
in what you have differed.

(3:55)

In this second passage the vague term translated "completing your term" (*mutawaffi-ka*) is usually taken to mean "cause you to die" (otherwise than on the cross). The unbelievers whom the followers of

Jesus are set above may be the Jews who did not accept him, and who are now in a subordinate position in the Byzantine Empire.

The first passage is directed against the Jews, and asserts that they did not kill Jesus. In a sense this is true, since the crucifixion was the work of Roman soldiers; and it is also true in a deeper sense, since the crucifixion was not a victory for the Jews in view of his resurrection. The words translated "it was made to seem to them" (*shubbiha la-hum*) are vague and can be translated in slightly different ways. A common interpretation among Muslims is that some other person, possibly Judas, was substituted for Jesus. The modern heretical sect of the Ahmadiyya hold that he only fainted on the cross, was taken down alive and recovered, and then went eastwards preaching; and they claim to have found his tomb in Kashmir. In the centuries before Muḥammad various heretical Christian groups tried to explain away the death on the cross in similar ways.[13] In recent years one or two Muslims have tried to find interpretations of the passage which would not contradict the Christian belief that Jesus really died.[14] The fact remains, however, that nearly all Muslims from the time of Muḥammad until today have taken the passage to mean that Jesus did not die on the cross. Thus their perception of Christianity includes the denial of what is central to all Christian faith.

The denial of the divinity of Jesus is made in several passages, and with it a denial of the doctrine of the Trinity. The chief passages are:

> O people of the Book, be not extreme in your religion,
> and speak of God only the truth.
> The Messiah, son of Mary, is only the messenger of God
> and his word which he placed in Mary
> and a spirit from him
> So believe in God and his messengers
> and do not say, Three.
> Cease; it is better for you.
> God is only one God.
> Far exalted is he above having a child.
>
> (4:171)

> Disbelieved have those who say,
> God is the Messiah, son of Mary.
> The Messiah said, O Banū Isrā'īl,
> serve God, my Lord and your Lord.
> Whoever gives partners to God,
> for him God has forbidden the Garden;

his abode is the Fire . . .
Disbelieved have those who say, God is the third of three;
there is no god but one God.

(5:76f.)

One time God said, O Jesus, son of Mary,
did you say to the people, Take me and my mother
as two gods apart from God?
He said, Glory to you; it is not for me
to say what I have no right to;
if I had said it, you would not have known . . .
I said to them only what you commanded me,
Serve God, my Lord and your Lord.
I was a witness to them, so long as I was among them;
and when you completed my term,
you were watcher over them.

(5:116f.)

It is clearly not necessary in the present context to discuss these passages in detail. The scholarly questions involved have been dealt with at length by Geoffrey Parrinder.[15] The Qur'ān gives no adequate account of the beliefs of the great majority of Christians in the time of Muḥammad, both of those in the Great Church and the Monophysites and Nestorians. The idea that Mary was one of the Trinity may have come from an obscure set of Collyridians, heard of in Arabia more than two centuries before Muḥammad. It is also possible that there was confusion due to the fact that in some Semitic languages the word for Spirit is feminine. The Qur'ān also seems to assume that Christians understood "son" in a purely physical sense, though when pagan Arabs were said to believe in "daughters of God" this may not have been taken physically.

In the case of Christianity as in that of Judaism it is important to notice how much is not said. There is no realization that Jesus was dealing not with complete unbelievers, but with people who believed in God and yet had introduced false emphases into their religious practice. For example, some insisted on the scrupulous fulfilment of ritual duties but were neglectful with regard to justice and to caring for others; and they also avoided dealings with those they labelled as sinners. It was to meet this last defect that Jesus asserted that in the case of the repentant sinner God not merely remits the penalties but restores him to favour. Again there is nothing in the Qur'ān about the primary work of Jesus, whether that is called the inauguration of the kingdom of God or the redemption of the world or by some other name. While it is stated that Jesus received from God a scripture called the Gospel (or Evangel – *Injīl*), there is nothing to suggest that this was any more like our actual gospels in the New Testament than the *tawrāt* received by Moses was like the actual Pentateuch. Indeed Muslims usually deny that our actual gospels are the book received by Jesus, since that consisted entirely of revelations from God and not of historical statements about Jesus.

There is a remarkable passage in which Christians are able to see a reference to the Eucharist:

> One time the disciples said, O Jesus, son of Mary,
> can your Lord send down for us a table from heaven?
> He said, Fear God, if you are believers.
> They said, We want to eat of it,
> and that our hearts may be at peace,
> and we may know you have spoken truthfully
> and be among the witnesses to it.
> Jesus, son of Mary, said, O God our Lord send down upon us
> a table from heaven, to be for us a festival,
> for the first of us and the last of us,
> and a sign from you: and give provision (of food) to us,
> for you are the best of providers.
> God said, I am sending it down for you.
>
> (5:112–15)

From this it would be impossible to gain any idea of the significance of the Eucharist for Christians.

THE FUNCTION OF INADEQUATE PERCEPTIONS

From the various passages quoted and the comments on them it is clear that for a modern person the Qur'ānic perception of Christianity is seriously inadequate and at some points erroneous. It is important, however, that the Christian of today should not take this as a reason for denying that Muḥammad was inspired by God. What is necessary, rather, is a reconsideration of the nature of prophethood. This is particularly necessary for Muslims, since according to the traditional Islamic view the Qur'ān is the very speech of God, and it is difficult to see how what appear to be errors can be attributed to God. The best solution of this problem for Muslims who are traditionally minded would probably be to say that God spoke in terms of what was believed in Mecca.

According to the leading Christian theologians today a prophet is a person who brings messages from God to the people of his own time and place. In so far as universal human matters are involved in this particular time and place, the messages will be relevant to a much wider circle of people, but in the first place they are for each prophet's immediate contemporaries. Jesus himself said, "I am sent only to the lost sheep of the house of Israel" (Matthew 15:24), but after his resurrection his followers soon discovered that his message was good news for Gentiles as well as Jews. Foretelling the future has often been regarded as an aspect of prophecy, but most prophetic predictions seem to consist mainly in pointing to the consequences of present conduct by way of punishment or reward. This matter will be discussed more fully in the next chapter.

The Qur'ān would seem to acknowledge its primary relevance to the Arabs of Muḥammad's time when it insists that is is an Arabic Qur'ān, and that prophets bring revelations in the language of their own people. The language of a people incorporates its whole way of thinking about the world and about human beings. Thus the Arabic word *ijāra* may be translated "the giving of neighbourly protection", but this English phrase conveys virtually nothing to those unfamiliar with the outlook and habits of the pre-Islamic Arabs. The verse "God gives neighbourly protection (*yujīru*), but no protection is given against him" (*lā yujāru 'alay-hi*) (23:88) cannot be understood by a westerner without much explanation. That is to say, God's revelation to a prophet is necessarily conditioned by the language and ways of thinking of the prophet and the people to whom the revelation is addressed in the first place.

In the light of this particularity of revelation the question of the inadequacy of the Qur'ānic perception of Christianity must be looked at more closely. It is certainly inadequate as a perception of the Christianity with which Muslims who have come to the west are in contact today. It is also an inadequate perception of the Christianity of the Byzantine Empire and other lands surrounding Arabia in the time of Muḥammad. But was it an adequate perception of the Christianity of those Christians with whom Muḥammad himself was in contact? To this question the answer is not simple. The question indeed has two aspects: factual truth and adequacy as a guide to action. Since we know virtually nothing about the precise views of the Christians living in Mecca or visiting it, we should allow that the

Qur'ānic perception of their beliefs may have been largely true. It would also appear that it was sufficiently true to be an adequate guide for Muḥammad in his dealings with the Christians of Mecca and with the Christian groups elsewhere in Arabia whom he encountered in the last two years of his life.

Muḥammad's treatment of Christian groups was closely bound up with his treatment of Jewish groups, since he was having problems with the latter as soon as he went to Medina. The beginning of his relationship with Jews and Christians goes back, of course, to the earliest years of his prophetic career, when he was assured by Waraqa that the revelations he was receiving were comparable to those received by Moses. The details vary in the different versions of the story about Waraqa, and this casts some doubt on it; but it would seem that Muḥammad must have had some external assurance from a qualified person that his experiences were comparable to those of Moses; those of Jesus were also mentioned at some point. As a result of this conviction Muḥammad expected, on going to Medina in 622, that the Jews there would accept him as a prophet, no doubt assuming that his message was almost identical with what the Jews believed. The Qur'ān had stated that it was confirming the previous revelations,[16] and the word translated "confirming" (*muṣaddiq*) means roughly "asserting the truth of" something. In Medina, however, a mere handful of Jews accepted Muḥammad as a prophet, while most not merely refused to accept him but made fun of his claims.

This is not the place to describe in detail Muḥammad's treatment of the Jews of Medina and other parts of Arabia. The crucial point appears to be that, because he based his claim to prophethood on the similarity of his prophetic experience to that of Moses and Jesus, he could not deny that Jews and Christians were people of the book, even if they had somehow deviated from what had originally been revealed to them, as he supposed. The Qur'ān produced many arguments against the Jews, and latterly also against the Christians. Most Muslims claim that the corruption of the Jewish and Christian scriptures was explicitly asserted in the Qur'ān, but in the next chapter it will be argued that this is not so, but that the doctrine is a dubious interpretation of some verses and was only worked out by Muslim scholars after Muḥammad's death. The main Qur'ānic perception of Jews and Christians may be said to be that they were people of the book, who had received scriptures proclaiming doctrines essentially the same as those of the Qur'ān, but that they had somehow come to deviate from the purity of scriptural truth, at least to the extent of not recognizing and acknowledging Muḥammad.

On the basis of this perception Muḥammad in his closing years initiated what developed into the system of "protected minorities" (*dhimmīs, ahl adh-dhimma*) within the Islamic state. Jewish and Christian groups were given a measure of internal autonomy under their religious leaders, provided they paid the taxes demanded of them, which were not unduly onerous. This policy of protected minorities was in accordance with traditional Arab ideas of the "protection" of weak tribes by strong tribes, but it also enabled the Muslims to avoid the almost impossible task of either converting all the Jews and Christians or expelling them from the territories under Islam. Where pagans and idolaters were given the choice of Islam or the sword, Christians and Jews could become protected minorities. In this way the Qur'ānic perception of Christianity, even if only partly true of the Christians of Muḥammad's time, provided the basis for a pragmatic solution of the problem of Christians within the Islamic state. In this respect the Qur'ān did add something to the previous perception of Christianity in Mecca.

After observing how this perception of Christianity, though inadequate in various ways, yet enabled Muḥammad and the early Muslims to frame a satisfactory policy towards Christians, the question of Muḥammad's prophethood may be looked at again. This is a matter on which it is important that Christians today should have a clear, positive view. To formulate such a view, however, is not easy because of the differences between the traditional Islamic conception of a prophet and that of the contemporary Christian. While for the Christian the prophet has a message from God for his own time and place, the Muslim tradition is that prophets receive the actual words of God without the admixture of anything human apart from the language, and that many of the revealed messages are of universal validity. It cannot be maintained that everything in the Qur'ān is universal, since it includes assertions about contemporary events such as the battles of Badr and Uḥud. In the eighth century the Nestorian Catholicos Timothy was prepared to say that Muḥammad "walked in the path of a prophet" though not that he was in fact a prophet, and this may be because he was aware of the Islamic conception of prophethood.[17]

Christians should begin to consider this question by looking at the historical background of Muḥammad's career and its historical outcome. As was seen in the previous chapter the Christianity of the time had a number of weaknesses. The Arabs of Mecca, owing to sudden economic affluence, found their old way of life breaking down, so that they required something like a new religion; but none of the existing forms of Christianity was able to meet their needs. In other words, there was a religious vacuum in Mecca which Christians could not fill. The subsequent acceptance of Islam by many in North Africa, the Fertile Crescent and Iran shows that there was something of a religious vacuum in these regions also. There are thus grounds for holding that God was behind the appearance of Islam in order to bring something better to the people involved. In other words, Islam came into being, not through human planning but by a divine initiative.

If a divine initiative is admitted, it has then to be asked how God worked through Muḥammad. In all my writing about Muḥammad, which began nearly forty years ago, I have always taken the view that Muḥammad was sincere in thinking that the Qur'ān was not his own composition, but came to him from beyond himself. I have therefore never used the words "Muḥammad says" of Qur'ānic assertions, though I have been accused of this, but have preferred the neutral phrase "the Qur'ān says". As long ago as 1953 I advocated the view that "the Qur'ān is the work of Divine activity, but produced through the personality of Muḥammad, in such a way that certain features of the Qur'ān are ascribed primarily to the humanity of Muḥammad".[18] More recently I have suggested that the revealed messages might be regarded as mediated by the unconscious of the prophet, though coming ultimately from God.[19] Such a view would help to explain features of the Qur'ānic perception of Christianity, but I would not insist on it. On the standard Islamic view that the Qur'ān is entirely from God, and that the personality of Muḥammad has contributed nothing, it is difficult to explain the inadequate and erroneous statements about Biblical matters. What is important here, however, is not to give any precise explanation of the "manner" of revelation in modern terms, whether speaking of the unconscious or of something else, but to insist that somehow or other the personality and world-view of Muḥammad entered into the revealed messages. Reference might be made to the case of the prophet Hosea in the Old Testament, for God showed Hosea that in his own experience of an unfaithful wife there was a parallel to God's experience of the unfaithfulness of his people Israel.

It is particularly important that the Christian of today should not allow the imperfect Qur'ānic perception of Christianity to blind him to the great positive values of Qur'ānic teaching, which are indeed the central truths of the Abrahamic religious tradition. God is the good creator of all human beings, who has made the world a suitable place for meaningful human life, and wants all human beings to believe in him; God will judge the moral quality of people's lives on the Last Day; God calls on all believers to worship him alone, to be grateful to him and to lead upright lives, especially by being generous with their wealth. The Qur'ān also presents Muḥammad as the person chosen by God to bring this message to the people of Mecca, to the Arabs, and then to a wider public. In the light of the great positive values of the teaching of the Qur'ān and the practical successes which resulted from it, the inadequate perceptions of Judaism and Christianity cannot be accounted a serious weakness, such as to negate all that is sound and true. It is a Christian principle that "by their fruits you shall know them",[20] and Islam has certainly brought to millions a better life than they would otherwise have had. It may even be said to have helped to make some Christian saints.[21]

> Massignon and Foucauld were both converted to Christianity by the witness of Islam to the one true living God. Someone wrote of Foucauld and of his devotion to the dead of Islam. For a mystic the souls of the dead count as much as those of the living, and his particular vocation was to sanctify the eternal Islam – that which has been and will be for eternity – in helping it to give a saint to Christianity.

Moreover there are many examples in Biblical and Christian history of how God is able to achieve his purposes through whatever instruments are at hand, even when they have some imperfections.

Christians should thus recognize a deep truth in the Qur'ānic claim to be following the religion of Abraham. Jews, Christians and Muslims all have a faith which goes back to that of Abraham, by whatever name it is called. While most Muslims seem to think that a religion has to remain static and unchanging, many Christians see religion as a living thing which grows and develops to meet the changing needs of human societies, and that it is only at its centre that there is something unchanging.

Chapter 3

The elaboration of Qur'ānic perceptions

During the caliphate of 'Umar (634–44) the Muslim armies conquered most of Syria, Egypt and Iraq, and the Christians there received the status of protected minorities, and were under no compulsion to become Muslims. This meant that the Muslims living in these provinces had opportunities of conversing with Christians, and some of the Christians were able to produce strong arguments against Islam by showing the discrepancies between the Qur'ān and the Bible. The Qur'ānic perception of Christianity, when applied in this situation, was clearly inadequate. It could not be abandoned, however, without rejecting the Qur'ān, and so Muslim scholars began to elaborate some aspects of that perception in such a way as to weaken the anti-Islamic arguments.

THE ALLEGED CORRUPTION OF THE SCRIPTURES[1]

One of the most important achievements of the early Muslim scholars was the development of the doctrine that at some unspecified point in the past the Jews and Christians had corrupted or altered their scriptures, so that these were no longer the real Torah and Gospel received from God by Moses and Jesus respectively. This made it easy for Muslims to rebuff any arguments based by Christians on the Bible. It was claimed that this doctrine of "corruption" or "alteration" (*taḥrīf*) was found in the Qur'ān, and there are in fact four passages where the word *yuḥarrifūna* occurs, which is a form of the verb which has *taḥrīf* as its verbal noun. An examination of these four passages shows that they do not contain anything like a doctrine of universal corruption. In the translation "alter" is used to render *yuḥarrifūna*.

Are you (Muslims) eager that they should believe in you,
when a group of them hears the speech of God and alters it,
then after understanding it (alters it) knowingly.
(2:75)

Of the Jews some alter the words from their sets,
and they say, We hear and disobey,
and, Hear something not heard,
and, Show regard for us,
twisting their tongues and slandering the religion.
If they had said, We hear and obey,
and, Hear, and, Consider us,
it would have been better for them and more correct.
But God cursed them for their unbelief,
so that except for a few they do not believe.
(4:46f.)

For their breaking their covenant we have cursed them,
and made their hearts hard.
They alter the words from their sets,
and they forget part of the admonition given them.
(5:13)

O Messenger, let not those grieve you who vie in unbelief,
of those who say with their mouths, We believe,
but whose hearts do not believe;
for of the Jews (are some) listening to falsehood,
listening to another people who have not come to you,
who alter the words after (being put in) their sets,
saying, If this is given you (by Muḥammad) accept it;
but if it is not given you, beware . . .
(5:41)

The vague phrase "alter the words from their sets" has been used deliberately because the Arabic word *mawāḍi'* can mean either "places" or "meanings". The last of the passages perhaps gives a slight preference to "places" as a rendering, since it is literally "alter the words after their sets", and this could be taken to mean "after (placing them in) their sets". The last of the passages is also somewhat mysterious, and no convincing account of its "conclusions" has been given in the commentaries;[2] but that is not relevant here. The point which it is important to notice is that this altering is something which is being done by the Jews of Medina who were Muḥammad's contemporaries, and the impression is given that what they were altering was only certain passages and not the complete Torah. Manuscripts of the Bible are still extant which antedate Muḥammad, but there is absolutely no suggestion in the Qur'ān that the whole Bible had been corrupted at some time in the distant past, nor that there had been the collusion between Christians and Jews which would have been necessary in order to corrupt the Old Testament.

It may also be noted that the examples given in 4:46f. are not quotations from the Bible, but seem to be verbal tricks played by the Jews of Medina on the Muslims. The first example appears to be making fun of the Muslims by using the similarity in sound between the Hebrew "we hear and obey" (*shāma'nū wa-'āsīnū*) and the Arabic "we hear and disobey" (*sami'nā was-'aṣaynā*). The second example is obscure and may be left aside. In the third the Qur'ān seems to want to stop the Jews saying "show regard for us" (*rā'i-nā*) because this resembles the Hebrew root for "evil" (*ra'*). There is nothing here about any corruption of the scriptures.

Another accusation made in the Qur'ān against the Jews of Medina was that they altered the text of the Torah when they recited passages from it to Muslims by "twisting their tongues" in it.

> One of them is a group who twist their tongues in the Book,
> that you may think it from the Book,
> though it is not from the Book, and saying,
> It is from God, though it is not from God,
> and speaking falsehood against God knowingly.
>
> (3:78)

They are also said to have copied it incorrectly when preparing copies for sale:

> Woe to those who write the Book with their hands;
> they say, This is from God, to buy a small gain.
> Woe to them for what they have written,
> and woe to them for what they have earned.
>
> (2:79)

It is possibly these alterations in reciting and copying which are referred to when the Qur'ān speaks about "inventing falsehood about God" in a number of passages.[3]

This appears to be the total amount of Qur'ānic material relevant to the question of the corruption of the Jewish and Christian scriptures. It gives no support to the view that these had been extensively corrupted in the ancient past before the time of our existing manuscripts, and yet this would be the only credible form of the view in the light of the manuscript evidence. There has so far been no detailed study of the way in which this doctrine of corruption was elaborated. Already the commentator Mujāhid (d.*c*.721), as reported by aṭ-Ṭabarī, seems to have taken the view that the verses with *yuḥarrifūna* implied the general corruption of the Torah.[4] Another early reference is in the report by the Catholicos Timothy on his discussions with the caliph al-Mahdī about 781.[5] The caliph spoke of a general corruption of the scriptures, and in particular mentioned the omission of passages foretelling the coming of Muḥammad as prophet. This would imply some alteration of the actual text.

Eventually there were two main forms of the doctrine of corruption. Some scholars maintained that there had been a wholesale corruption of the text, a view that was expounded and defended at length by Ibn Ḥazm (d.1064).[6] Other scholars, however, took a milder view and held that it was not the text but only the interpretation that had been corrupted. This was apparently the view adopted in the "Refutation of the Christians" by al-Qāsim ibn Ibrāhīm (d.860). There were also some intermediate views. This lack of agreement on what precisely was meant by corruption did not matter. It was sufficient to be able to say to a Christian "your scripture is corrupt" and that parried any argument.

THE ASSUMPTION THAT MUḤAMMAD WAS FORETOLD IN THE BIBLE

Muḥammad and the early Muslims believed that Muḥammad's coming as a prophet was foretold in the Bible. The Qur'ān asserts that Muḥammad was the messenger and prophet "whom they will find written (or described) in the Torah and the Gospel which they have" (7:157). There are also a number of passages in which the Jews are accused of concealing the truth or concealing part of the scriptures, or are told not do do so,[7] and these were probably originally understood as concealing prophecies of the coming of Muḥammad. The caliph al-Mahdī, in talking to Timothy, insisted that there were three passages which clearly foretold Muḥammad. One was the passage in Deuteronomy 18:18 in which God promises to the Israelites that he will raise up from their brothers a prophet like Moses. Another was the "rider on a camel" of Isaiah 21:7 (which some contemporary scholars think should in fact be a plural); and the third was the promise of the Paraclete or Comforter in the New Testament.[8]

Christians understand this foretelling of the coming of the Paraclete as referring to the Holy Spirit (as is explicitly stated in John 14:26). At some point, however, the similarity was noticed between two Greek words, *periklutos* meaning "famous" or possibly "praiseworthy" and *paraklētos* or Paraclete; and this became the basis of a claim that what Jesus had said about the Paraclete really referred to Muḥammad, whose name means "praised".

At this point it is necessary to go back to the Qur'ān to look at an important verse there:

> One time Jesus, son of Mary, said
> O Banū Isrā'īl, I am a messenger of God to you
> confirming what I have of the Torah
> and announcing a messenger coming after me
> whose name is *aḥmad*.
> But when he came to them with the Evidences,
> they said, This is magic clear.
>
> (61:6)

From about the middle of the eighth century the word *aḥmad* has been taken as a proper name which is an alternative for Muḥammad. Up to that time, however, it would appear that *aḥmad* was regarded as an adjective meaning "more praiseworthy", but of course still referring to Muḥammad. It is noteworthy that even in 781 al-Mahdī in talking to Timothy does not take it as a proper name.[9] I have called attention elsewhere to the curious fact that until about AD 740 no Muslim boys were called Aḥmad, whereas after that date it became very common as an alternative for Muḥammad.[10] The wording of this Qur'ānic passage suggests that already in Muḥammad's milieu there may have been an awareness of this confusion between *periklutos* and *paraklētos*; and of course in a Semitic script, using only consonants, they would be identical, *prklts*.

My suggestion that until the eighth century the word *aḥmad* in this verse was taken as an adjective is supported by various other facts. Thus, in his biography of Muhammad, Ibn-Isḥāq (d.768) speaks of the verse in question, but does not mention Aḥmad as a name of the Prophet.[11] This passage is remarkable in that Ibn-Isḥāq gives a fairly accurate translation of John 15:23–16:1, apart from replacing "whom I will send you from the Father" with the words "whom God will send you from the Lord". Actual translations from the Bible are unusual in Muslim writers. In introducing the quotation Ibn-Isḥāq says it is "from what the disciple John set down for them when he wrote down for them the Gospel from the testimony (*'ahd*) of Jesus, son of Mary, in respect of the Messenger of God". For Ibn-Isḥāq the point of the quotation is his claim that the term *manḥamannā*, which he uses for "paraclete" in it, is a Syriac word meaning *muḥammad*, and is equivalent to the *baraqlītis*. It would be out of place here to discuss the Syriac ramifications of this argument.[12] The point to be noted is that the Muslims were firmly convinced that Muḥammad had been foretold in the Bible.

Elsewhere in Ibn-Isḥāq and in the *Ṭabaqāt* of Ibn-Sa'd (d.844)[13] there are numerous stories about the ways in which the Jews and Christians concealed the passages foretelling Muḥammad. Sometimes there was physical concealment by sticking pages together or by obliterating a verse or putting one's hand over it.[14] Such stories would seem to be intended for simple-minded illiterate people. Stories that the Jews were expecting a prophet may derive from expectations of a Messiah. Best known is the story of the Christian monk Baḥīrā who, while Muḥammad was on a trading journey to Syria, recognized from descriptions in his books the seal of prophethood between his shoulders, and told his uncle Abū-Ṭālib to look after him carefully.[15]

By the eighth century some Muslim scholars were searching the Bible for further verses which could be claimed as foretelling Muḥammad. This, of course, implied the soundness of the Biblical text and contradicted those forms of the doctrine in which the whole text was unreliable. A well-known scholar, Ibn-Qutayba (d.889), found a considerable number of such verses, but he was surpassed by a convert from Christianity, 'Alī ibn-Rabbān aṭ-Ṭabarī (not to be confused with the historian-exegete), who produced no less than 130.[16]

Christians today, who think that a prophet's message is primarily for his own time and place, would look differently from the Christians of New Testament times at messages foretelling the future. Today's Christians would allow that prophetic messages may refer to the future in two ways. First, a prophet could call the attention of his contemporaries to disasters that would come upon them as punishment for particular sinful behaviour; such disasters were to be expected in the near future. Second, the prophetic messages may contain statements of the general ways in which God deals with human beings, both punishing the sinful and supporting the upright and delivering them from adversity; and the supportive actions need not happen immediately.

The passage in Deuteronomy 18:14–19 in which Moses says to the Israelites that God will raise up for them from among their brothers a prophet like himself seems to state a general principle, namely, that when God's people need divine guidance or other help God will send a prophet to give them that. This principle could be taken to be fulfilled in the whole series of prophets who through many centuries guided the Israelites. The later Jews thought it applied to the coming of the Messiah, and it was taken in this sense by the early Christians and applied to Jesus (Acts 3:22f.). From this standpoint a Christian can admit that in a sense it also applies to Muḥammad. At the same time, however, it has to be pointed out that today's Christians do not regard the fulfilment of this prophecy in some person as a proof of his prophethood; whether he is truly a prophet is known from the quality of the messages he delivers and their fruits in the lives of his followers.

It should also be noted that the modern way of thinking about prophethood does not set any store by accidental resemblances between prophetic passages and later events. Thus there is a passage in Isaiah which reads:

> (The sign) is this: The young woman will conceive
> and bear a son, and will call his name Immanuel.
> Butter and honey will he eat, so that he may know
> how to refuse the evil and choose the good.
> For before he knows how to refuse the evil
> and choose the good,
> the land you abhor will be forsaken by its two kings.
> (Isaiah 7:14)

(Modern scholars also understand the last clause differently.) The ancient Greek version of this text has "the virgin" although the Hebrew, followed here, has a word meaning "young woman" which may even refer to one recently married. Early Christians familiar with the Greek text saw this verse as foretelling the virginal conception of Jesus, and Immanuel is regarded as one of his names. According to the modern understanding of the verse it is telling the king of the time, Ahaz, that within a few years disaster will overtake his enemies. The name Immanuel or "God with us" emphasizes a general principle and assures the king of God's constant support; but it is also very appropriate to Jesus once the verse has been applied to him. Thus for the modern Christian the application to Jesus does not prove anything, and in a sense is no more than a curious accident; but it has a firm place in Christian history since it is part of the way of thinking of the early Christians. In calling this accidental it is implied that it is not part of God's practice to cause prophets to utter cryptic sentences whose meaning will only become clear centuries later.

Christians do believe, however, that the passion and death of Jesus are foretold in the Old Testament, but that this falls into the category of general statements about how God deals with human individuals and communities. One such statement is the description of God's suffering servant in Isaiah 52:13–53:12. While this is seen to apply specially to Jesus as Messiah, there is a sense in which everyone who sets out to do an important piece of work for God may have to face suffering and death. It seems obvious to an outsider that those Muslims today who are endeavouring to gain acceptance for what they regard as a truer conception of Islam than that of the fundamentalists will almost certainly have to face great suffering.

MUSLIM PERCEPTIONS OF WORLD-HISTORY

It was shown in Chapter 2 that in pre-Islamic Arabia there was little understanding of history or the historical process. The Qur'ān insisted that there had been many previous prophets, but gave the impression that the communities to which they brought a message were isolated from one another and that their religious belief had not lasted for any length of time, though the religion of Abraham had continued as far as his great-grandchildren. The one exception to this discontinuity was the tribe-like community of the Banū Isrā'īl, to which first Moses had gone, then other prophets, then Jesus; but there was no clear idea of the linkage between the various events mentioned in the Qur'ān or of the continuity of Israelite history. Moreover, when the Qur'ān described events in past religious history, it did so in an allusive way, as if its audience already knew something about the events. By the time of the second or third generation of Muslims there were demands for fuller descriptions of the various events and incidents, and also for some knowledge of how they were related to one another.

To meet the first demand there was a class of popular preachers or story-tellers (*quṣṣāṣ*), who produced colourful and greatly expanded versions of the Biblical and other stories referred to in the Qur'ān.[17] Some of this material they obtained through oral contacts with Jews and others, but where material was scarce they gave free rein to their imagination. Among the *quṣṣāṣ* were those whose knowledge was fairly sound, but others were unscrupulous and used dubious sources which they supplemented lavishly. As a result the jurists and other serious scholars felt threatened by the *quṣṣāṣ*, and tried to regulate and limit their activity. There were also persons who produced the desired material at a scholarly level. One of the best known of these was the Yemenite convert from Judaism, Ka'b al Aḥbār (d.638).[18] Another important scholar was Wahb ibn-Munabbih (d.732), apparently not a convert, but with the reputation of having read seventy of the older books. He is said to have written *Kitāb al-mubtada'*, and this may be one of the chief sources of the book about to be mentioned.[19]

In the course of 1989 an American scholar, Gordon Newby, published an important book entitled *The Making of the Last Prophet: A Reconstruction of the Earliest Biography of Muhammad.*[20] The title is slightly misleading because what Newby reconstructs is only the first of three parts of the *Sīra* of Ibn-Isḥāq, called *Kitāb al-mubtada'*, "The Book of Beginnings" or Genesis. This contains extended accounts of the earliest prophets mentioned in the Qur'ān, but has nothing about Muḥammad himself. Ibn-Isḥāq's chief editor, Ibn-Hishām, omitted the whole of *Kitāb al-mubtada'* from his recension of the *Sīra*, and no manuscript of it exists. Quotations from it, however, have been preserved by other authors, notably by aṭ-Ṭabarī in his history and Qur'ān commentary, and it is these which have been collected and translated by Professor Newby. Most scholars will be surprised to discover how extensive these quotations are. They have been arranged in chapters, one for each of the prophets, and are placed in the order in which they come in aṭ-Ṭabarī's history. It is reasonable to assume that this was the order given to them by Ibn-Isḥāq. If this assumption is correct, it means that Ibn-Isḥāq – or perhaps a predecessor such as Wahb ibn-Munabbih – had undertaken the task of providing a chronological order for the events mentioned in the Qur'ān.

To show how far the Muslims still were from having a true perception of Judaism and Christianity it will be useful to look at this book more fully. The list of chapters is as follows:

> Creation, Adam and Eve; Noah and his issue; Hūd; Ṣāliḥ; Abraham, the Friend of God; Lot; Job; Shu'ayb; Joseph; Moses; Ezekiel; Elijah; Elisha and successors; Samuel; David; Solomon; Sheba; Isaiah; al-Khidr; Daniel, Hananiah, Azariah, Mishael, and Ezra; Alexander; Zechariah and John; the family of 'Imrān and

Jesus son of Mary; the Companions of the Cave; Jonah; the Three Messengers; Samson; George.

There are here some glaring mistakes in chronology. Jonah and Samson are placed after Christ; in the case of Jonah his father's name Amittai may have been confused with Mattai or Matthew. Ezekiel, who is not mentioned by name in the Qur'ān, is brought in to explain a verse (either 2:259 or 2:243), but the story given has nothing to do with the real Ezekiel and is placed in the time of the Judges shortly after Joshua. Hūd, Ṣāliḥ and Shu'ayb are Arabian prophets. Sheba is an Arabian tribe which perished because of its unbelief (54:15–17). The Queen of Sheba, known in Arabic as Bilqīs, comes into the story of Solomon. Samuel is not named in the Qur'ān, but there is a reference to him in 2:246. There is nothing about Isaiah in the Qur'ān, but some obscure verses (17:4–8), which speak of the Banū Isrā'īl twice going astray and becoming liable to punishment, are referred to him here, together with the abortive attack of Sennacherib on Jerusalem.

Al-Khidr, a mythical Arabian figure, usually identified with "one of our servants" in 18:65, who gave instruction to Moses, is taken by Ibn-Isḥāq to be Jeremiah, and this gives him an opportunity to speak of the destruction of Jerusalem and the Exile. In 18:83–98 there is a mysterious person called Dhū-l-Qarnayn who is given power and a commission by God, and Ibn-Isḥāq accepts the usual identification of him with Alexander the Great, but has few genuine historical details. After the time of Christ come the Companions of the Cave, who belong to Christian legend, the unnamed Three Messengers of 36:13–29, and the Christian martyr George, about whom there is nothing in the Qur'ān.

There is not a great deal in Ibn-Isḥāq about Mary and Jesus. In accordance with the passage 3:35–44 Zechariah is for a time Mary's guardian; and when he finds himself incapable of fulfilling his duty of maintaining her, she is entrusted to a carpenter called George. She is secluded in a church, and there is joined by a youth called Joseph, and they help one another in such matters as fetching water. There is no mention of an older man Joseph as her husband, though later she is described as a widow. The account of the birth of Jesus follows the Qur'ān, 19:16–34 (quoted in the previous chapter), but adds that it took place at Bethlehem, and that beside the palm tree there was a manger. In a short account of the events leading to the crucifixion it is stated that the place of Jesus was taken by a man called Sergius.

There is an account of the tomb of Jesus being found at Medina, though it is also held, in accordance with the Qur'ān (3:55; 4:158), that God took Jesus up to himself.

In his introduction to the translations Professor Newby emphasizes that Ibn-Isḥāq was illustrating and developing the Qur'ānic conception of a series of prophets and the myth or, as I would prefer to say, image of prophethood. Much of Ibn-Isḥāq's material can be traced to extra-biblical Jewish sources, and a small amount to Christian sources other than the New Testament, while there are a few stories whose source has not been identified. Despite the translation from the Fourth Gospel mentioned on p. 34, Ibn-Isḥāq does not in general appear to have had access to a copy of the Bible. Where he reproduces Biblical material, he attributes it to "the people of the Torah" or "the people of the (first) Book", and this would seem to imply that he received it orally. For some matters he mentions Wahb ibn-Munabbih as a source.

Some further information about Christianity is found in the third part of Ibn-Isḥāq's *Sīra* in connection with the sending of envoys by Muḥammad to various rulers. In a kind of parenthesis there is a list of eleven disciples sent by Jesus to various peoples, though there is no mention of Mark being sent to Egypt.[21] Then there are accounts, omitted by Ibn-Hishām, of how the Byzantine Emperor Heraclius and the Abyssinian Negus believed in Muḥammad's prophethood.[22]

After the phenomenal conquests of the first century of Islam, which created an empire stretching from Spain and Morocco in the west to Central Asia and the Punjab in the east, there gradually developed a vision of the future of world-history. This was basically the expectation that the process of conquest would continue until the whole world had been converted to Islam. One of the ways in which this vision was expressed was by regarding the world as divided into two spheres, the sphere of Islam and the sphere of war (*dār al-islām, dār al-ḥarb*). The former was where a Muslim was ruling according to Islamic law, and the latter was where that was not yet the case. It was possibly in order to strengthen this way of seeing world-history that the verse (33:40), which spoke of Muḥammad as "the seal of the prophets" (*khātam an-nabiyyīn*), came to be interpreted as meaning that he was the last of the prophets after whom there would be no other. To some of the earliest Muslims, however, this phrase may have meant no more than that he was the seal confirming the previous prophets, as was frequently stated in the Qur'ān. By taking it to assert that there would be no prophet after him, Muslim scholars implied that the

Qur'ān was, as it were, God's last word to the human race, so that the community of Muslims was intended eventually to include everyone except those destined for Hell.

This conception of the two spheres has had a prominent place in Muslim thinking ever since. Such events as the expulsion of the Muslims from Spain, finally completed in 1492, were seen as temporary setbacks. The Ottoman successes in eastern Europe in the sixteenth century appeared to be a renewal of the expansion of Islam; but even the loss of territory by the Ottomans between the eighteenth century and the end of the First World War did not lead to complete abandonment of the conception, and some of the more enthusiastic supporters of Imam Khomeini and other fundamentalist leaders seem to think that a new period of advance is beginning.

ISLAMIC SELF-SUFFICIENCY

Though I have more than once called attention to the significance of the story about the library of Alexandria told by Edward Gibbon in his history of the Roman Empire (Ch. 51), it makes an important point so succinctly that it is worth repeating. When Alexandria was conquered in 641, the victorious Arab commander wrote to the caliph 'Umar in Medina asking what was to be done with the famous library. He received the reply, "If the books are in accordance with the Qur'ān, they are unnecessary, and may be destroyed; if they contradict the Qur'ān, they are dangerous and should certainly be destroyed." The story comes, of course, from a Muslim source. Gibbon was somewhat doubtful of its accuracy, and modern historians think that the library had moved away from Alexandria before the Muslim conquest. Yet even if its facticity is rejected, the story expresses an attitude that has determined the perceptions of Muslim scholars through the centuries, and still does so. They believe that Islam is the final religion since Muḥammad is the last prophet, and that in the Qur'ān and Ḥadīth (anecdotes about Muḥammad) Islam possesses in essentials all the religious and moral truth required by the whole human race from now till the end of time. Hence in the religious and moral sphere Islam has nothing to learn from any other system of thought.

Along with this story another story is worth considering which may well be true. An early scholar with leanings to sufism, al-Ḥārith al-Muḥāsibī (d.857), wrote a *Refutation of the Mu'tazilites* (a sect regarded as heretical by mainstream Sunnism) and was severely criticized by the slightly older scholar, Aḥmad ibn-Ḥanbal (d.855), founder of the Ḥanbalite legal school and rite. What Ibn-Ḥanbal criticized was that al-Muḥāsibī, before refuting the heretical doctrines, had given a full and presumably objective account of them; and Ibn-Ḥanbal was afraid that someone might read the false doctrines and accept them without looking at the refutation.[23] This attitude of trying to prevent people from even hearing false doctrine has been prominent in the practice of Muslim ulema through the centuries. It seems to show a distrust of the ability of the ordinary human mind to distinguish between truth and falsehood. Possibly this is linked with the belief that the truth of revelation is supported not primarily by reason but by the miracles vouchsafed by God to the prophet who proclaims the revelation.

The result of this general attitude has been that Muslim ulema, the official religious scholars of Islam, have constantly tried to prevent ordinary Muslims from gaining any knowledge of false or heretical doctrines. When Muslim scholars wanted to write books about the Muslim sects, it was necessary for them, before they did so, to justify their enterprise by claiming that they were explaining and illustrating a statement of Muḥammad's about the seventy-three sects of Islam.[24] In a similar way Muslims have shown no interest in studying doctrines of other religions. There were indeed one or two exceptions to this in medieval times,[25] but it is only in the last couple of decades that Islamic universities have begun to study comparative religion.

At the root of this attitude is a conception of knowledge different from that of most westerners. For the traditionalist Muslim, knowledge is essentially religious and moral knowledge, or, as I have called it elsewhere, "knowledge for living", and this is really all contained in the Qur'ān and Ḥadīth. For the westerner, on the other hand, knowledge is mainly "knowledge for power", namely, knowledge about the natural world and about human individuals and communities, since this knowledge makes it easier to control things and people.[26] It is probably the assumption of self-sufficiency rather than belief in the corruption of the Bible that has kept Muslims from studying it. A western Christian may think that the Book of Mormon is valueless in itself, but, if he had frequent contacts with Mormons, he would spend a little time studying it in order to understand better the people he was dealing with. It is thus difficult for a westerner to appreciate this Muslim fear of exposure to false teaching. Yet this fear helps to explain the urgency of the campaign to have Salman Rushdie's book banned and burnt.

There are a number of Ḥadīth and stories of early Muslims which serve to enforce the principle that it is undesirable to have religious discussions with Jews and Christians. When the caliph 'Umar came to Muḥammad carrying a Jewish or Christian book, the latter was angry and said to him:

> Are you all amazed about them (? these books), O Ibn-al-Khaṭṭāb? By God, they were brought to you white and pure; do not ask them (these people) about anything; they will tell you something true and you will disbelieve it, or something false and you will believe it. By God, even if Moses was alive, nothing would be open to him but to follow me.

The early Qur'ānic scholar Ibn-'Abbās is reported to have said:

> How do you ask the people of the Book about anything while your Book, which God revealed to his prophet, is among you? . . . Did God not inform you in his Book that they have changed and altered (*ghayyarū*, *baddalū*) the Book of God, and have written the Book with their hands and said, This is from God, that thereby they may make a small gain (2:79)? Does he not forbid you the knowledge that comes from questioning them? By God, we never saw a man of them asking you about what God revealed to you.

This statement implies that the Muslims already have all sound religious knowledge; and in another statement Ibn-'Abbās told people to make the Qur'ān the test of truth and falsity: "If you are asking them, that is that; but see what agrees with the Book of God, and accept it, and what is contrary to the Book of God, and reject it."[27]

Another aspect of this attitude towards what is not Islamic is to be seen in the gradual rejection of Isrā'īliyyāt. These were primarily materials derived from Jewish converts to Islam, such as Ka'b al-Aḥbār and Muḥammad b. Ka'b al-Quraẓī, though ancient material was sometimes included.[28] At first this material had been acceptable, and there is a Ḥadīth, quoted by ash-Shāfi'ī (d.820), in which Muḥammad said that there was no objection to transmitting stories from the Banū Isrā'īl.[29] In course of time, however, objection was taken to the Isrā'īliyyāt, and it was generally held that they were to be avoided.

Early this century the prominent Egyptian scholar, Rashīd Riḍā, who advocated a return to the pure Islam of "the pious ancestors" (*as-salaf aṣ-ṣāliḥ*), attacked some of the improbable stories found in medieval commentaries on the Qur'ān. He tended to reject anything that was not from an Islamic source, and in particular criticized some of the stories where Ka'b and Wahb ibn-Munabbih were named among the transmitters. Other scholars opposed Rashīd Riḍā and pointed out that Ka'b and Wahb had been accepted as sound transmitters by early authorities on Ḥadīth like al-Bukhārī (d.870). To this Rashīd Riḍā replied that some of the stories derived from Ka'b and other Jewish converts were even in contradiction to the Old Testament. His opponents had to admit this, but claimed that later story-tellers had put their own fantastic inventions into the mouths of Ka'b and Wahb. Eventually a moderating view seems to have prevailed which has been described as follows:

> When *isrā'īlīyāt* on the authority of Ka'b, Wahb or others agree with the Qur'ān, they constitute a *ḥuǧǧa*. When they are at variance with the Qur'ān, they should be considered spurious. When they fall outside the scope of the Qur'ān, they should be neither believed, nor disbelieved, mindful of the prophetic saying: "Do not believe the people of the Book and do not accuse them of falsehood."[30]

The opening sentences here are reminiscent of 'Umar and the library of Alexandria.

Throughout the centuries the ulema have used their authority to prevent the dissemination of all heretical or non-Islamic views, and indeed of whatever deviated from their own teaching and from the Islamic self-image as they conceived it. The suppression or squeezing out of undesirable views has been carried out by methods not unlike those of western totalitarianism. In some Islamic countries at the present time it is virtually impossible for Muslim intellectuals to publish anything at variance with the dominant fundamentalism or traditionalism.

LATER PERCEPTIONS OF WORLD-HISTORY

It will be instructive at this point to look at the works of three medieval Muslim historians. These will provide evidence of the tendency to neglect everything non-Islamic and in particular the historical background of Judaism and Christianity. At the same time some genuine information about Christianity filters through.

The first of the works to be considered is the world-history of aṭ-Ṭabarī (d.923). A summary of the contents of the first thousand pages of this work shows how interest was focused first on matters spoken of in the Qur'ān, and then on the background of the numerous converts to Islam in Iraq and Iran.[31]

	no. of pages
The nature of time; beginning and end of world; God eternal and creator	21
The beginning of creation; Iblīs	57
Adam and Eve	80
From Seth to birth of Noah	18
Noah	17
Kings of Yemen	29
From Noah to Abraham	21
Abraham, and foreign kings in his time	73
Lot	18
Death of Abraham; his descendants	17
Job, etc.	10
Jacob and his sons; story of Joseph	43
Moses, etc. (kings of Babylon)	92
Joshua	10
Qārūn (a Qur'ānic figure)	11
Kings of Babylon	6
Israelites after Joshua; Elijah and Elisha; Samuel and Saul	24
David and Solomon	38
Persian kings of Babylon	22
Israelites after Solomon to Nebuchadnezzar	52
Affairs of Babylon, Yemen, etc.	19
Restoration of Jerusalem	1
Persian kings, Alexander and successors	49
Included in above:	
Zechariah and John	11
Mary and Jesus	5
Roman kings ruling Syria from Christ to Muḥammad	3
Various Arab tribes before and after Christ	31
Companions of Cave, Jonah, Three Messengers, Samson, George	36
Kings of Fars (Persia)	over 200
including: birth of Mary	11

This summary speaks for itself. The account of the Roman emperors (here called kings of Syria) is no more than a list of names with figures for the number of years reigned. By way of exception there is a brief reference to the crucifixions of Peter and Paul under Nero and to the destruction of Jerusalem under Vespasian and Titus. There is no mention of Constantine becoming a Christian. One significant point is that just before this list of kings aṭ-Ṭabarī has an account of Mary and Jesus, and, after reproducing Ibn-Isḥāq's mainly Qur'ānic version of the birth, has another version which gives further matters from the New Testament.[32] Among these are: the coming of envoys from the king of Persia with gifts for the Messiah; Herod's plot to kill him; the command to a man called Joseph (though not designated as Mary's husband) to take her and the child to Egypt; and their return to Nazareth. There is thus slightly more knowledge of the standard Christian account of the nativity, though mixed with erroneous ideas, but at the same time there is still a vast area of which the great historian is ignorant.

The work of al-Mas'ūdī (d.956), *The Meadows of Gold*, is conceived of as entertainment rather than pure history.[33] In the early volumes there is much geographical material along with accounts of the curious habits and customs of the various peoples and races. The following list gives some idea of the contents of the first two volumes, though the headings are only approximately correct, since much extraneous matter is included under each:

	no. of pages
(vol. 1) From the creation to Noah	37
Abraham to Solomon	29
Rehoboam etc.; destruction of Temple; Samaritans; John the Baptist (1); Mary and Jesus (1)	12
Indian history (and other matters)	31
Various geographical matters	188
China and the Turks	39
Geographical matters	77
(vol. 2) Kings of Syria, Mosul, Babylon, etc.	27
Earlier and later kings of Persia, etc.	137
Alexander and successors	51
The Romans; Augustus and the pagan emperors	18
Constantine, etc.; church councils; Nestorians and Jacobites	22
Christian emperors since Islam	23
Egypt	87

Here again we see much greater interest in the early rulers of Iraq, Iran and Syria than in the background of Christian history. There is nothing about the pre-Christian history of the Greeks and Romans. His interest does, however, extend to India, China and the Turks of Central Asia; and he apparently breaks fresh ground by giving some information about the Romans and Byzantines after the time of Christ.

Somewhat inexplicably he has a completely erroneous account of John the Baptist. He is said to have preached to the Jews, who opposed him and put him to death, and then a king called Herod took vengeance on the Jews for his death. Previously Ibn-Isḥāq knew that John had been put to death by Herod for criticizing an incestuous marriage, but got most of the details wrong. Al-Mas'ūdī has fuller information, however, about Jesus. He knows that he was born at Bethlehem on Wednesday 24 December (a point he must have got from contemporary Christians), and makes no mention of the Qur'ānic palm tree. Then, after describing how Jesus studied the Jewish religion as a boy, he recounts an incident which apparently happened when he was in a synagogue. He found "traced in characters of light" the words, "You are my son and my beloved; I have chosen you for myself", and then went on to claim that "today the word of God is fulfilled in the son of man". This seems to reflect an incident in the synagogue at Nazareth, except that the quotation from Isaiah comes elsewhere in the gospels.[34] After saying that he has visited a church in Nazareth al-Mas'ūdī speaks briefly of the call of the disciples, though mentioning only the four evangelists by name, then of the baptism of Jesus, of his miracles and of his passion. Most interesting, however, is his concluding statement, which implies some knowledge of the New Testament. He says:

> In the Gospel there is a long discourse about the Christ and Mary and Joseph the carpenter; but we leave this aside, since God most high has not spoken of any of this (in the Qur'ān) nor has Muḥammad (on him be peace) spoken of it.

Several hundred pages later al-Mas'ūdī comes to the Romans. He has some trivial details about the Emperor Augustus, and mentions the birth of Christ during his reign, then his death under Tiberius. He says the persecution of Christians began under Claudius, but is not sure whether the martyrdom of Peter and Paul was in this reign or that of Nero. He then speaks of the spread of the Christian faith through the work of various apostles, notably Mark in Egypt. He also names the four evangelists, and identifies the "three messengers" of sura 36 with Peter, Thomas and Paul. Then comes a list of most of the emperors up to Constantine, but the only facts mentioned, apart from their being idolaters, are matters of interest to Christians, such as the destruction of Jerusalem and its restoration, the persecutions and the death of the disciple John (in the reign of Trajan!). The story of the Companions of the Cave is inserted here.

Al-Mas'ūdī next deals with the Christian emperors of the Romans in some detail. He describes the conversion of Constantine, and the founding of churches in Palestine and elsewhere by his mother Helena. He has brief accounts of six ecumenical councils and of the rejection there of the views of the Nestorians and Jacobites (among whom he includes the Copts), but the views are not spelled out. One of his incidental remarks is that it was Christians who brought about the decline of the sciences of the Greeks (Murūj ii, p. 321). In the period after Muḥammad military relations with the Islamic Empire attract most attention. Altogether his knowledge of Christianity shows remarkable advances on what was known to aṭ-Ṭabarī. If any part of the Bible was accessible to the latter, he may have avoided consulting it, because as a jurist he would believe in its corruption; but al-Mas'ūdī has no such scruples. Besides referring to the Gospel, as noted earlier, he mentions the Torah and the book of Baruch, son of Neriah, though what he claims to derive from the latter, does not occur in the deuterocanonical book of that name.

Another book which will be noticed here is *The Perfection of History* (*al-Kāmil*) by Ibn-al-Athīr (1160–1234), which became a standard work for later Muslim scholars.[35] For the period to AD 900 it is mainly an abridgement of aṭ-Ṭabarī though with some additions. He follows the earlier historian exactly in making Jonah, the Three Messengers and Samson post-Christian, but differs in some of the stories he relates about Jesus. Joseph the carpenter plays a more prominent part, but he is spoken of as a relative, not as Mary's husband. There are stories of how Jesus as a young boy helped to detect a thief, and also of how, when he was falsely accused of murdering a boy, he brought the corpse to life for a short time, so that it could give evidence on his behalf and reveal the real murderer. The story of the birth of Jesus is close to the Qur'ān and does not speak of a manger under the palm tree. After mentioning a version in which the birth took place in Egypt he adds that the first version of the birth in the land of Mary's people is more accurate. Nevertheless at another point he accepts the view that Mary's pregnancy lasted, not nine or eight months, but only one hour, on the ground that this is closer to the Qur'ān where it says that "she conceived him and retired with him to a distant place" (19:22).

Where aṭ-Ṭabarī held that the person crucified in place of Jesus was called Sergius, Ibn-al-Athīr favours the view that it was his betrayer, Judas, though he mentions another possibility – a name that looks like Natlianus. He adds little to the previous account of the earlier Roman Empire, but apart from Constantine onwards has some additional details and mentions five ecumenical councils. All this, however, gave Muslims very little idea of the historical background of their Christian protected minorities, and still less of the Byzantine Empire. Perhaps the significant point is that in the period between aṭ-Ṭabarī and Ibn-al-Athīr little attempt had been made to discover more about this background. Indeed, it would seem to be only in the twentieth century that a few Muslims have tried to gain a more accurate understanding of Christianity and its history.

This lack of interest in everything other than Islam and the Islamic world is not surprising when one remembers the picture of world-history developed by Muslim scholars out of Qur'ānic perceptions. Since Muḥammad was the final prophet and Islam the final religion, the historical process must be moving towards the ultimate triumph of Islam throughout the world. This meant that Christianity would probably fade away completely, or else remain as a group of insignificant minorities within the Islamic Empire; and from this it followed that it was pointless to have any real knowledge of Christianity, even if it had been possible to distinguish between what was true and what was false in the Christian scriptures and Christian teaching. The expansion of the Ottoman Empire in the fifteenth and sixteenth centuries doubtless strengthened this conviction. It does not seem to have occurred to any Muslim intellectuals that one could handle opponents better when one had some accurate knowledge about them.

The lack of interest in Christian history is doubtless also to be connected with the general attitude to history found among many Muslims. Such historical knowledge as the pre-Islamic Arabs had was chiefly of the glorious deeds and famous victories of their own ancestors. A natural development of this was the interest shown by Muslim scholars in recording the achievements of Muḥammad and succeeding generations of Muslims, especially their successes on the field of battle. History became a recognized field of study. About the fourth Islamic century, however, as Sir Hamilton Gibb has noted, a change took place. Up to that point the Muslim chroniclers were applying some principles of historical criticism to their materials and making advances in historical method; but they they found themselves unable to resist pressures from the ulema, who by this time had reconstructed the history of early Islam on a dogmatic basis, and who had come to regard history as primarily "an instrument of moral instruction and dogmatic controversy". Gibb describes this as the "subordination of historical method and thought to the demands of religious emotion and theological dogma".[36] The presentation of Islamic history by the ulema came to be "invested with religious sanctions, so that to question it came to be regarded as heresy". This was doubtless why al-Mas'ūdī refrained from setting down things he had read in the gospels. Even the new stories of the miracles of Jesus found in Ibn-al-Athīr's account was material which confirmed the traditional Islamic idea of prophethood and its place in world-history.

Islamic historians suffered from not having a clear chronological basis. Though from Muḥammad's Hijra events were dated by years, they had no equivalent for our BC (or BCE). The reason for aṭ-Ṭabarī's list of Roman emperors from Augustus was probably mainly chronological, but not much use was made of this. The historians seem to have thought rather in terms of eras. Thus al-Mas'ūdī gives a list of eras with the length of each in years at one point in his book.[37] The turning points are: Adam; Noah and the flood; Abraham; Moses and the Exodus; the founding of Solomon's temple; Alexander; the birth of Christ, or his "raising" or ascension; Muḥammad (Hijra or death). From Solomon's temple to Alexander he gives 717 years, which is too long; and from Christ to Muḥammad he has three figures (from different points) of 521, 546 and 594 years, which are not too far out. Nebuchadnezzar appears at all sorts of dates. Ibn-al-Athīr has a report that Nebuchadnezzar destroyed Jerusalem because of the killing of John the Baptist, but rejects this since he thinks that his attack was because of the killing of Isaiah.[38] This shows how important it is to remember that the early Islamic historians lacked many of the basic tools of the modern historian.

The modern westerner cannot but be aware of the shortcomings of the Islamic view of world-history, but he should not allow this to blind him to certain basic truths which it enshrines. The idea of the primordial covenant between God and the posterity of Adam means that the human race has a central place in the purposes of God, and that a large part of it is destined to come finally into a conscious relationship with God, serving him and worshipping him, both in this world and in the world to come. For the realizing of this purpose God has sent countless prophets; and the westerner could see in these all those who have contributed to the development of the greater and lesser religions of the world. Such persons have brought to their fellows some knowledge of God and his universe, even though it is not in identical or even comparable terms to the formulations of the Abrahamic religions.

As a final thought it might be suggested that when Christians feel aggrieved at seeing how their religion was being neglected and treated as of little value by the Muslims in their colonialist days, they should be asking themselves whether in their own colonialist days they have not neglected and treated as of little value Islam and the other religions of their subject peoples.

Chapter 4

The encounter with Greek philosophy

The encounter of Islam with Greek philosophy is not part of its encounter with Christianity, but it is relevant to that in various ways. It has been suggested by western scholars that one of the decisive moments in the history of Islamic civilization was its rejection of the Greek philosophical thinking which was to become of primary importance in the development of European civilization, and that this rejection made it more difficult for Islam to come to terms with the latter. This suggestion has a superficial attractiveness, but it raises issues which require to be examined closely. In this chapter I endeavour to deal with these issues, while realizing that my competence does not extend to all the matters involved.

MUSLIM ATTITUDES TO GREEK PHILOSOPHY

As a result of the early conquests, especially that of Iraq, the Muslims by the middle of the eighth century were in contact with a living tradition of Greek thought. In Iraq there were Christian schools or colleges, using Syriac as the medium of instruction, where Greek medicine, philosophy and other sciences were studied. Muslim rulers soon became interested in Greek medicine and astronomy particularly – the latter was useful in determining the direction of Mecca, which had to be faced in prayer. Until 870 the court physician of the 'Abbāsid caliphs was a Christian. Early in the ninth century the caliph al-Ma'mūn established a library and centre for translating Greek books, and eventually the works of some eighty Greek authors became available in Arabic.[1] A decade or two earlier a few Muslim theologians became interested in Greek philosophical and scientific conceptions, and began to use some of these in their arguments against adherents of other faiths and against Muslims with whom they disagreed. This use of Greek conceptions also owed something to former pupils of the Christian schools who had become Muslims. Two of the earliest theologians to be interested in Greek conceptions were Hishām ibn-al-Ḥakam and Ḍirār ibn-ʻAmr, both of whom flourished from about 780 to 800.[2]

This use of Greek conceptions by early theologians led to the development of the discipline of Kalām, philosophical or rational theology. Among the exponents of this was the theological school or sect of the Muʻtazilites. These discussed all the problems with which contemporary Islamic theology was concerned, but differed from the main stream of Sunnite theology on a number of points, such as believing in the freedom of the human will in contrast to divine predestination. As a result they were adjudged heretics. About 900, al-Ashʻarī (873–935), who had been trained as a Muʻtazilite, left the sect and went back to the main stream, but continued to use the methods of Kalām which he had learnt in order to defend traditional doctrines.[3] He was not the only thinker to do this, but after about the year 1000 his name was given to the main school of Sunnite Kalām in the central lands of the caliphate. A comparable school in the east, the Māturīdites, did not achieve real prominence until centuries later. The early practitioners of Kalām were content with a limited number of Greek philosophical and scientific ideas, and apparently little was added to these by the theologians until the time of al-Ghazālī.

Meanwhile, however, there were a number of Muslims who were prepared to go much further even than the Muʻtazilites in their acceptance of Greek thought. These came to be known as the Falāsifa (the plural of the Arabic *faylasūf* or *philosophos*). One of the earliest was al-Kindī (*c*.800–*c*.868), an Arab by birth, about whose thought unfortunately not much is known.[4] Another was the Persian Abū-Bakr Muḥammad ibn-Zakariyyā' ar-Rāzī (d.923/32), whose book *The Spiritual Physick* has been described by the translator into English as expressing an attitude of "intellectual hedonism".[5] More important was al-Fārābī (*c*.875–950) who defended what he regarded as standard Islamic views on a Neoplatonic basis. His philosophical position was further refined by Ibn-Sīnā or Avicenna (d.1037), who is one of the world's great philosophers. Although these Falāsifa have an important place in any general history of philosophy, they had little influence in the Islamic world of their own days. The standard Muslim theologians did not discuss their views even to refute them, and the works of the philosophers had currency only among their immediate followers, though some of their ideas seem to have penetrated the more educated sections of the community, and were perhaps gaining ground there.

This was the position when al-Ghazālī (1058–1111), as a relatively young man of 33, was appointed professor at the prestigious Niẓāmiyya college in Baghdad. His teacher al-Juwaynī (d.1085) had alerted him to the threat to mainstream theology from the Falāsifa. It would have been impossible for him to go to any teacher of philosophy, but he obtained copies of the works of Avicenna and others, and through private study so mastered these that he was able to produce an account of Avicenna's philosophy (*Maqāṣid al-falāsifa*, "The Aims of the Philosophers") which some reckon to be more lucid than anything by Avicenna himself. After this, however, he wrote a refutation of these teachings (*Tahāfut al-falāsifa*, "The Inconsistency of the Philosophers").[6] In this he maintains that on three points they had ceased to be Muslims, namely, in denying a bodily as distinct from a spiritual resurrection, in holding that God knows only universals and not particulars, and in holding that the world had existed from all eternity. There were also seventeen points on which he deemed them heretical. Al-Ghazālī was also interested in showing the extent to which some of the sciences of the Falāsifa, such as mathematics, had nothing in them contrary to Islamic doctrine and so could be accepted. In particular, he wrote introductory textbooks on Aristotelian logic with examples suited to the needs of Muslim theologians.[7]

One of the results of the work of al-Ghazālī was that some later theological treatises had extensive sections dealing with philosophical preliminaries. This may be illustrated by looking at the distribution of contents in one of the best-known treatises, the *Mawāqif* of al-Ījī (d.1355); with its commentary by al-Jurjānī (d.1413) it fills four large volumes.[8] The six sections are as follows: the object and methodology of Kalām; being and non-being, the possible and the necessary, cause and effect, etc.; accidents, quality, quantity, relations, etc.; substance, bodies, souls; the being, unity, attributes and acts of God; prophethood, eschatology and other "traditional" matters. Thus nearly two-thirds of the treatise and commentary is concerned with philosophical preliminaries to the theology proper. Something similar is already seen in the *Muḥassal* of Fakhr-ad-dīn ar-Rāzī (d.1210), though in this case the preliminaries occupy only about half of the work.[9] Several other similar treatises are described by Louis Gardet and Père Anawati in their introduction to Islamic theology.[10] The important question which these examples raise is whether it is correct to speak of the rejection of the Falāsifa as a complete rejection of Greek thought by Muslim theologians, or whether one should not say that they accepted it and adapted it to their own needs. Before deciding this point, however, it would be helpful to look at what happened in western Christendom.

Al-Ghazālī's critique of Avicennian philosophy did not completely stop philosophizing among Muslims. In the east there was no great name after Avicenna, who had died in 1037 over twenty years before al-Ghazālī was born, but a philosophical theosophy has continued to the present time. In the Islamic west, on the other hand, the twelfth century saw perhaps the greatest of the Arabic Falāsifa, Ibn-Rushd or Averroes (d.1198). He had a legal training and for most of his life served as a judge, but he was also well versed in the Greek sciences. In particular, he studied Aristotle and wrote commentaries on some of his works, correcting many of the Neoplatonic misinterpretations current among the Falāsifa. He also wrote a refutation of al-Ghazālī entitled "The Inconsistency of the Inconsistency" (*Tahāfut at-Tahāfut*).[11] Despite his eminence he had no successors in the Islamic west and was hardly known in the east. Although he was a qāḍī (judge), he suffered a measure of repression at times from the traditionalists. Perhaps his greatest achievement was the reintroduction of the genuine Aristotle to the western Europeans.

WESTERN CHRISTIAN ATTITUDES TO GREEK PHILOSOPHY

The living tradition of Greek philosophy in the Byzantine Empire played an important part, as was noted on p. 2, in the formulation of Christian doctrine at the ecumenical councils. As a result of the barbarian invasions, however, and the breakdown of the Western Roman Empire, little intellectual culture was left in western Europe. There had been a certain revival of intellectual life at Seville under Isidore (d.636), but this largely faded away after the Arab invasion. Even the tenth century showed little sign of intellectual life in western Europe apart from commentaries on a few logical works of Aristotle. Round about 1100 Anselm was using dialectical methods to defend Christian doctrine, and in this he was followed in a more sophisticated way by Peter Abelard.

A change gradually came about, however, because after the Christian conquest of Toledo in 1085 many learned Muslims and Arabic-speaking Jews continued to live there, and Christian scholars from many countries went to Toledo. During the twelfth century a vast number of philosophical works were translated from Arabic into Latin,[12] and these led to a new surge of intellectual activity in western Europe, affecting science and philosophy as well as theology. One line of the thinking of Averroes was taken up by Siger of Brabant (*c.*1235–82) and others, who came to be known as the Latin Averroists. Averroes had argued that, since both philosophy and the revealed scriptures are true, there cannot be any disharmony between them, and he had gone on to attempt to show in detail how apparent contradictions can be reconciled. The Latin Averroists accepted the basic principle, but paid little attention to reconciling contradictions, so that their theory came to be known as that of "double truth" and to be adjudged heretical.

The main influence of Averroes is to be seen in the Dominicans Albertus Magnus (*c.*1206–80) and Thomas Aquinas (1226–74). These largely accepted Aristotelianism as expounded by Averroes, and then Aquinas in particular made it the basis of an all-embracing metaphysical and theological system, which is generally regarded as the high point of western Christian thought in the Middle Ages, even though there was some Christian opposition to it.

Further classical Greek works became known in western Europe after the Ottoman capture of Constantinople in 1453 and the flight of eastern scholars westwards, but there was no slavish imitation of the Greeks. The turmoil of the Reformation in the sixteenth century probably tended to focus minds on theology; and by the seventeenth century profound new movements of thought were making their appearance.

FURTHER REFLECTIONS

This chapter opened with a suggestion about the apparent rejection of Greek philosophy by Islam, but, if we now turn back to that matter, we are at once confronted with the further question whether there is any essential difference between the attitude of men like Fakhr-ad-dīn ar-Rāzī, al-Ījī and al-Jurjānī and that of Thomas Aquinas. Sir Hamilton Gibb, in discussing the point, noted that what both Muslim and Christian thinkers were saying was very remote from the outlook of the ordinary man.[13] This is true, but the point may be left aside here, since even ordinary men usually want to know that those who are their intellectual superiors are capable of defending the faith intellectually. Gardet and Anawati, who talk about the *conservatisme figé* of the Islamic theology of the last few centuries, at one point suggest that the rigidity is due to the fact that the Muslim scholars were only defending accepted formulations of dogma, not trying to reach a deeper understanding of the realities involved;[14] and there may well be some truth in this.

My instinct, on the other hand, is to see the difference between the final results in Islam and Christianity as due to the attitudes of the authorities in both religions to statements of doctrine. In Christianity the most notorious case was the silencing of Galileo in 1633. As early as 1543 Copernicus had made public his theory of the universe, according to which the earth moved round the sun and not, as had hitherto been supposed, the sun round the earth. It was only in 1616, however, after the support of this theory by Galileo, that it was condemned, and Galileo was told neither to hold it nor defend it. In 1632, however, he published a book which his opponents claimed to be a defence of the Copernican theory, and for this he was condemned, though he avoided punishment by recanting. It has been suggested by recent students of the period that the opposition to him was as much from philosophers as from theologians, presumably because his theory contradicted that of Aristotelian science.

The ban on Copernican views by the religious authorities in Rome had only a limited effect. The intellectual life of western Europe was now flowing through many different channels, of which Catholic theology was only one. Some of the Protestant authorities tried to exercise control, but only over theological doctrines, while there were many men devoting themselves to various branches of science. This intellectual diversity was doubtless an important factor in freeing western European thinkers from religious and other forms of control. In most countries it was possible to have books published, even when they expressed views contrary to the established religion of the country; and when this was not possible, the books could often be published in another country.

The philosophical opposition to Galileo points to a distinction which has to be made within Greek thought, namely, that between particular philosophical doctrines and the general attitude of following the argument wherever it leads. It was this latter which was the more important Greek contribution to the world. When Aristotelian philosophy became closely associated with Christian dogma in the Thomist system (especially as it had been revived in the sixteenth century by Jesuits and others), there seems to have been a tendency to regard philosophy as also producing a form of dogma not to be questioned. By the seventeenth century, however, numbers of people were becoming deeply interested in science, and were prepared to carry on their researches and their theorizing despite ecclesiastical opposition. In England, in particular, scientific work was encouraged by the Royal Society, which included many Anglican clerics among its members. For the upholders of science and the new philosophy of Descartes and Locke, Thomism and other forms of scholasticism seemed to be dictatorial and authoritative, hidebound and unimaginative.[15]

This look at the relation of philosophy and theology in western Europe gives a better perspective from which to review the position in Islam. Although al-Ghazālī produced what was perhaps a devastating critique of the Falāsifa, he was far from rejecting philosophy as such. Indeed what he achieved was at least a partial adoption of philosophy into Kalām. Superficially considered, there seems to be little difference between the attitude to philosophy shown in the later works of Kalām and in that of Thomas Aquinas, though this is a topic which could benefit from further investigation. What can be said, however, is that, just as philosophy had become somewhat fossilized in the Jesuit and other schools of Galileo's time, so it became fossilized in the main Islamic schools after about the fifteenth century. In other words, Greek doctrines were accepted to a large extent, but there was no sign of the Greek openness to following the argument. It was probably the repressive and suppressive measures of the ulema which led to the decline of philosophy in the Islamic east after Avicenna and to its disappearance in the Islamic west after Averroes. It was probably also the attitudes of the ulema which led to the decline of the pursuit of science among the Muslims.[16] Thus the inability of Islam to deal with the thinking of modern Europe is due not to its rejection of the particularities of Greek thought, but to its rejection of the Greek openness to new truth.

Chapter 5

Encounters under Muslim rule

It was shown in a previous chapter how, when Muslim scholars elaborated the Qur'ānic perception of Christianity, they were making an initial response to the needs of Muslims living intermingled with Christians. As the centuries rolled on, this intermingling continued in the various Islamic states, and both Muslims and Christians took defensive measures of one kind or another. These will now be looked at. First, however, it will be helpful to describe the extent and character of Islamic domination – the Dār al-Islām.

ISLAMIC COLONIALISM

When Muḥammad died in 632, the Islamic state in embryonic form, together with its allied tribes, controlled much of Arabia. Under the second caliph 'Umar (634–44) a phenomenal expansion began, which continued for about a hundred years. Westwards by that time the Muslims ruled most of Spain and the whole of North Africa from Morocco to Egypt. Northwards they occupied Syria, and Damascus was the capital of the Umayyad dynasty (661–750); but they had not managed to settle permanently in Asia Minor owing to the strength of the Byzantine Empire. Eastwards the Sassanian (Persian) Empire had quickly collapsed, and the Muslims then swept through Iraq and Iran to Central Asia (Bukhara, Samarkand) and the Punjab. This was the extent of the Islamic Empire during the last decade or two of the Umayyads, and expansion after that was only sporadic.

This section has been headed "Islamic colonialism" because in the last half-century Muslim apologists have come to complain about what they call European colonialism, alleging it to have been almost invariably hostile to Islam. It is thus important to remind Muslims that there have been times in past history when Muslims have been an aggressive imperial or colonialist power. Some of the modern apologists try to maintain that Islamic expansion was not colonialist, because the primary aim of the Muslims was not territorial, but to bring the benefits of the Islamic religion and polity to those unfortunates outside the sphere of Islam. (One is reminded of "the white man's burden" and the bringing of the benefits of Christianity, with European culture, to the benighted people of Africa and Asia.) The contention of the apologists is not supported by the Arabic sources. It seems clear that the military expeditions which led to the expansion of the territory under Muslim rule were basically raids in a quest for booty. This point will be better understood if one goes back and notes what was happening during Muḥammad's lifetime.

That part of the biography which deals with events from his Hijra or emigration to Medina in 622 until his death in 632 is called *Kitāb al-maghāzī*. The *maghāzī* are sometimes called expeditions, but a better term would be razzias, which is a Europeanized form of another Arabic word from the same root and with the same meaning. The razzia or raiding expedition was a regular activity of nomadic Arab tribes. It consisted in making a sudden unexpected descent on an isolated group of men pasturing camels or other animals of a hostile tribe, and then driving off the animals. If the attacking force was much larger, it was no disgrace for the herdsmen to run away. Mostly there was no loss of life, and so the razzia was almost a form of sport for the bedouin. As more and more nomadic tribes became allies of Muḥammad, he realized that he could not allow his allies to raid one another, and must therefore find some other outlet for the energies they had been putting into the razzia. Thus in his closing years he organized what might be called glorified razzias along the routes to Syria and Iraq.[1] The continuation of this policy under the caliph ʻUmar led to pitched battles between Muslim and Byzantine or Sassanian armies, in which the Muslims were nearly always victorious.

Nomadic tribes and more settled groups which had suffered from Muslim raiders soon realized that they could avoid attack by submitting to the Islamic state. For Christian and Jewish groups this meant accepting the status of protected minorities; for others it could be some form of alliance together with acceptance of Islam. As more and more groups became incorporated into the Islamic Empire in one form or another, it was necessary for the raiding expeditions to go further afield in the search for booty. There seems to have been at least one expedition almost every year in the campaigning season, but it became virtually impossible to return to Medina after each campaign. For the non-campaigning season camp-cities were established in places such as Cairouan in Tunisia and Basra in southern Iraq, and it was to these that the armies returned after their campaigns. The expedition of 732 into France, which was defeated at Tours (or, as the French prefer to say, Poitiers), was such a raiding expedition, and the result of the battle was to show the Muslims that raiding in that direction was no longer profitable.

The administration of the Empire so rapidily acquired was greatly facilitated by the system of protected minorities, which has already been described. Groups of Jews, Christians, Zoroastrians and even Hindus could become protected minorities (in the later Ottoman Empire "millets") with a measure of autonomy under their religious head – rabbi, patriarch, etc. The religious head dealt autonomously with the internal affairs of the group according to their own laws. They paid taxes to the governor of the province, but these were not excessive. On the whole Muslim colonialist regimes behaved very fairly towards their minorities and did not oppress them. The worst that could happen was that in a time of crisis a mob could get out of hand and attack minorities, but this was rare. Apart from this, however, the members of the minorities always felt that they were second-class citizens, excluded from the Muslim élite and from many government positions. Moreover, while a Muslim man could marry a woman from the minorities, a man from the minorities could not marry a Muslim woman.

This is a suitable point at which to mention the condition of Christianity in North Africa. Under the Roman Empire until about the fifth century there had been a flourishing Christian population in the provinces along the southern coast of the Mediterranean. It is likely that the Christians were mostly found in the Roman towns near the coast, and that there were few Christians further inland. One gets the impression, however, that by the time of the Arab advance in the second half of the seventh century there were few Christians left. Towards the middle of the fifth century there had been a Vandal invasion, and the Vandals were Christians following the Arian heresy, who persecuted non-Arians. After the defeat of the Vandals by a Byzantine general in 534 there were incursions by pagan tribes from the interior. All this reduced the number of Christians, since, apart from the actual loss of life, many seem to have fled to Italy or Spain. There are records of small Christian communities until the sixteenth century, but they were so small and insignificant that they cannot be said to have played any part in Muslim–Christian encounter.[2]

The unity of the Islamic empire was not maintained after the fall of the Umayyad dynasty of caliphs in 750. The ʻAbbāsid dynasty which replaced them and moved the capital to Baghdad never extended its rule to Islamic Spain. After about a century and a half, too, they lost control of many provinces. Strong provincial governors with the backing of powerful armies demanded that a son should succeed them, and the caliphs were forced to appoint the son as their next governor. In 945 even Iraq and Baghdad had to be yielded to such a person. In this way the Islamic Empire came to be ruled by dynasties of warlords, who gained some legitimacy from being nominally appointed by the caliph of the day, but sometimes determined the sphere of their rule by fighting other warlords. The caliphs had no longer any political power, but only a primacy of honour and some legal responsibilities. This state of affairs lasted until the conquest of Baghdad by the Mongols in 1258. After that there was no generally recognized caliphate, though in about the seventeenth century the Ottoman sultans claimed to have inherited it.

After what might be called a flirtation with the Muʻtazilite heresy in the early ninth century the ʻAbbāsid caliphs from 848 were upholders of the Sunnite form of Islam, as were the Ottoman sultans later. In 909 a family professing Ismaʻīlite Shīʻism gained control of Tunisia and in 969 conquered Egypt. This is known as the Fāṭimid dynasty, and Cairo was founded as their capital. They did not recognize the ʻAbbāsid caliphs, but carried on propaganda against them. They continued in power until 1171, when they were replaced in Egypt by Saladin and the Ayyūbids, who were Sunnites. In the centuries after the fall of Baghdad in 1258 three empires played an important role in the Islamic world: the Mogul (Mongol) Empire in India, which was at its height from 1556 to 1707; the Ṣafavid Empire and its successors in Iran; and the Ottoman Empire in the Middle East (about which more will be said in a later chapter). What is remarkable is that throughout all these political changes the fabric of Muslim society remained relatively stable, a fact which is in itself a tribute to the excellence of the social system established on the basis of the Islamic Sharīʻa; and this system included the acceptance of non-Muslims as protected minorities. There was indeed an Islamic colonialism, but it was a relatively benign form of colonialism.

MUSLIM POLEMIC AND APOLOGETIC

The Qur'ān had criticized Jews and Christians for their exclusiveness, and had further criticized Christians for holding that Jesus was divine, for believing in three gods and for asserting that Jesus died on the cross. Actual contact with Christians led to further points of criticism. Ibn-Isḥāq has a story about the visit to Muḥammad of a deputation of Christians from Najrān in the Yemen.[3] Two of their leaders spoke to Muḥammad, and he said to them, "Submit" (as *muslims* to God – *aslimā*). They claimed that they had done so, but he retorted that this was false, since they asserted that God had a son, worshipped the cross and ate pork.

As noted earlier, Muslims were discouraged from having discussions with Christians. As an exception, however, a Christian called Timothy, the Catholicos or head of the Nestorians in Iraq, had two days of discussion with the caliph al-Mahdī in the year 781. Timothy wrote an account of this in Syriac, which was translated into Arabic, and more recently into English.[4] This gives considerable insight into the state of the dialogue between the two religions at that time. In general, the caliph asked questions and Timothy replied. Some of the issues raised by the caliph seem to be petty verbal points, but others show some understanding in depth. Among minor questions are why Christians face east in worship, why they worship the cross, and why they are not circumcised. As the discussion follows a somewhat irregular course, it will be convenient to collect the caliph's main points under a few headings. Something will be said about Timothy's arguments in the next section.

The caliph began by accusing the Christians of believing that God married a woman and begat a son, and later asked how begetting could be possible without genital organs. He also insisted that Jesus cannot be divine, since the eternal cannot be born in time. He quoted the phrase "I go to my God and your God" (John 20:17), and referred to Jesus worshipping God and praying. His complaint that Christians put the creator and the servant on the same footing does not necessarily show any knowledge of New Testament references to Jesus as a "servant" (*doulos*), but may refer to the Qur'ānic description of him as *'abd* (the slave or worshipper of God). Timothy frequently speaks of Jesus as the Word of God, and to this the caliph cannot object since the term is used in the Qur'ān, though he insists that the word is created (as is also the Spirit of God). The caliph also holds that, if Jesus died, this shows he is not God, since God cannot die. There are long, rather unhelpful, discussions of the doctrine of the Trinity. The caliph firmly maintains that this means three gods, but nowhere suggests that Mary is one of the three (as in the Qur'ān) or objects to the statement that the three are Father, Word or Son and Spirit.

The references in this and the following paragraph are to the English translations in *Woodbrooke Studies*, ii. The caliph repeats the allegation that the Jews and Christians have corrupted the scriptures (35, 56–8), though the chief defect seems to be that prophecies of the coming of Muḥammad have been removed. He is also aware that there are four gospels, and asks about how they came to be written down (47–9, 60). He specifically mentions that the promise in the gospel of the coming of the Paraclete refers to Muḥammad (33–5), as well as that to the Israelites of the coming of a prophet like Moses from their brothers (50ff.), and the phrase about the rider on a camel from Isaiah (21:7), which Timothy takes to refer to the fall of Babylon to Cyrus (37ff.).

There are some long arguments about the use of corporeal or anthropomorphic terms in respect of God (70–2, 78–80). Both parties have to admit their use, but each tries to show that its own use is justified and that of the other is not. This discussion arises in part out of a comparison of the threefold character of God with the threefold character of the human person (soul, mind, reason). Then there is another long argument about God perceiving himself eternally (73–7). These are the most subtle parts of the whole conversation.

This account of the meetings of the caliph and the Catholicos is in many ways a fascinating document, but it is clearly not what is nowadays understood as dialogue. Each of the participants is arguing in terms of an intellectual structure which supports his faith, and defending that against criticisms; but there is no real sharing of religious experience.

The Arabic text of what purports to be a discussion by letter between a Muslim and a Christian in the reign of the caliph al-Ma'mūn (AD 813–33) was published in London in 1880.[5] The Muslim, 'Abd-Allāh ibn-Ismā'īl al-Hāshimī, described as a relative of the caliph, invites the Christian to accept Islam and so escape from Hell. The Christian, 'Abd-al-Masīḥ ibn-Isḥāq al-Kindī, a Nestorian, then gives a fuller reply, occupying about six-sevenths of the volume; Georg Graf and other recent European scholars think that both the setting of the exchange of letters and the names of the writers are fictitious, and that the work may have been written a century or more after the ostensible date. The Muslim's letter only briefly mentions the Qur'ānic criticisms of the doctrines of the Trinity and incarnation, as well as the worship of the cross, and it contains a virtually complete list of the books of the Bible. Since it is unlikely that any Muslim in the early ninth century would have had such a list, it may well be that this letter also was written by the Christian author.

Numerous works of anti-Christian polemics by Muslims have been preserved, and it would be pointless to attempt here a survey of them all.[6] It will be sufficient to mention one or two authors.

Among examples of anti-Christian polemics from the ninth century is a "Refutation of the Christians" (*Radd an-Naṣārā*) by the well-known writer al-Jāḥiẓ (d.868).[7] Possibly a little earlier is "The Book or Religion and Empire" (*Kitāb ad-dīn wa-d-dawla*) by 'Alī ibn-Rabbān aṭ-Ṭabarī, who appears to be a convert from Christianity, and whose list of alleged Biblical prophecies of Muḥammad has already been mentioned. He also lists a large number of alleged miracles of Muḥammad.[8] Manuals of theology, such as those of the Ash'arite theologians al-Baqillānī (d.1013)[9] and al-Juwaynī (d.1085),[10] include some subtle arguments against Christians and other non-Muslims.

In the eleventh century in Islamic Spain there appeared a book which is of great importance for the understanding of Muslim anti-Christian polemic. This is the *Kitāb al-Fiṣal* of Ibn-Ḥazm (d.1064), which contains refutations of the views of non-Muslim philosophers and Muslim heretical sects, as well as of those of Jews and Christians.[11] In the first section dealing with Christianity (i.48–65) he describes Christian answers to Muslim criticisms, such as the argument that, since God is living and knowing, he has life and knowledge, and that his life is the Spirit and his knowledge the Son; in response to this argument he points out that there are many other attributes which can be asserted of God, such as power, generosity, sight, speech and wisdom, and that in one passage Paul speaks of Jesus as the power of God and his knowledge.[12]

Ibn-Ḥazm knows something of the differences between Melchites (or Orthodox), Jacobites and Nestorians, including the differences between the one-nature Christology of the Jacobites and the two-nature Christology of the others. Against those who hold that there are two natures in Christ, humanity and divinity, and that it was only the humanity that was crucified and died, he argues that it follows that it was only half of Christ that died (62). What appears to be a fresh criticism of Christianity is that the distinctive practices, such as the observance of Sunday (instead of the Jewish sabbath), their fasting, their festivals, their omission of circumcision and their permission to eat pork, are prescribed nowhere in the gospels. He even knows that Jesus said, "I came not to alter anything of the rules of the Torah" – a free rendering of Matthew 5.17.

From what has been said so far it is clear that Ibn-Ḥazm had a fuller knowledge of many Christian matters than his predecessors. From a later section of his book (ii.2–75) it appears that he had had in his hands a copy of the New Testament and possibly one of the whole Bible. He speaks of the Jews as having prophecies from Moses, Joshua, Samuel, David and Solomon (the last two being presumably the books of Psalms and Proverbs), but rejects the later prophetic books, perhaps because they did not fit into the Qur'ānic conception of prophethood (ii.4). He gives a complete list, however, of the books of the New Testament, together with the number of pages in each. He also knows something of the history of the four gospels, presumably what was believed by Christians in his time.

Ibn-Ḥazm uses all his knowledge, however, to produce what he regards as devastating arguments against the Christians. He starts from the position or assumption that Jesus had received from God a Qur'ān-like scripture, and then proceeds to show that little of this has been preserved in the actual gospels. These are historical works composed by their writers, whose sources, such as the apostle Peter, he tries to identify, in order to discover whether they could have preserved the genuine scripture revealed to Jesus. In this he is trying to show that the gospels have no chains of transmitters comparable to those for the Islamic Ḥadīth. With regard to the Pauline epistles he notes the short time Paul was in contact with Peter, suggesting that he could only have an imperfect knowledge of what Peter could bear witness to. He also notes that for three hundred years until the conversion of Constantine the Christians were persecuted and had no secure place for their documents. Later he moves on to mention contradictions or alleged contradictions between the four gospels, and to argue that this proves they are completely untrustworthy. The conclusion is that, while Muslims are required to honour the revelation received by Jesus, they cannot be certain that any part of the gospels is a true recording of this revelation. In other words the Christian scriptures are completely corrupt.

In all this the modern western scholar cannot but note that Ibn-Ḥazm, despite his much greater knowledge of Christianity, had no interest in obtaining a deeper understanding of the Christian religion, but was only concerned to defend his Islamic faith and the perception of Christianity derived from the Qur'ān and the subsequent elaborations. While something of this attitude may be due to Ibn-Ḥazm's personal characteristics, it may also be partly due to the troubled times in which he lived. He was born in 994, and his father, and he himself in the first part of his life, had positions in the administration of the Umayyad rulers of Islamic Spain. This was a very unsettled period, however, because Umayyad rule, after flourishing for two centuries, was now disintegrating. It finally collapsed in 1031, and was replaced by a number of smaller political units known as the "reyes de taifas" or "party kings" (*mulūk aṭ-ṭawā'if*). Ibn-Ḥazm himself was in prison more than once. In writing about religions and sects he was probably moved chiefly by the dangers facing the Islamic establishment rather than by any awareness of the growing threat from the Christians in the north; but he certainly writes as one who is very much on the defensive. The net result of all his study and writing was not a better understanding of Christianity, but a strengthening of the very inadequate perception of Christianity.

A work of a rather different kind may be looked at briefly. This is a refutation of the divinity of Jesus ascribed to the well-known al-Ghazālī.[13] Though it was accepted by Louis Massignon as a genuine work of the theologian, later studies make it virtually certain that it was not by him.[14] There are strong grounds for thinking that the author was a Coptic convert to Islam, since at one point he quotes in Coptic the phrase "and the Word was made flesh" from the opening of the fourth gospel. This book also differs from most of the Muslim polemical writings in that it makes no mention of a corruption of the Christian scriptures, and is prepared to accept the phrase "son of God" as metaphorical. The main thrust of the argument is to show that various phrases in the gospels, which Christians take to imply the divinity of Jesus, do not have this implication if properly interpreted. There are also criticisms of Christian explanations of the Trinity and of the union of humanity and divinity in Jesus.

Al-Ghazālī himself in his genuine works shows little interest in Judaism and Christianity, and this is not surprising, since most of his life was spent in Baghdad or eastern Iran where opportunities for contact would be few. In one of his minor works he imagines a Muslim being distressed if asked to repeat the Islamic profession of faith substituting the name of Jesus for that of Muḥammad – there is no god but God, Jesus is the messenger of God" – and then he goes on to point out that this assertion is perfectly acceptable, and that Christians err only in respect of two matters, namely, holding that "God is the third of three" and denying the prophethood of Muḥammad.[15] In his greatest work, the *Iḥyā'* ("The Revival of the Religious Sciences") al-Ghazālī quotes a number of sayings of Jesus relevant to the life of a sufi; and in his book on the names of God he has a sympathetic discussion of the conception of "incarnation" (*ḥulūl*) in connection with the sufi idea of "becoming characterized with the characters of God" (*at-takhalluq bi-akhlāq Allāh*).[16] In all these genuine works the attitude of al-Ghazālī is in sharp contrast to that of Ibn-Ḥazm.

An objective scholarly attitude towards Christianity is shown by ash-Shahrastānī (d.1153). He was a theologian of the Ash'arite school, and like al-Ghazālī was well versed in philosophy. The text of a theological Summa with an abbreviated English translation was published in 1934.[17] He is best known, however, for his book on sects, *Kitāb al-milal wa-n-niḥal*, which was published in London in 1842 and shortly afterwards translated into German.[18] It deals not only with the Islamic sects but also with other religions and with the philosophers, Greek and Islamic. There is a lengthy account of the philosophy of Avicenna. The general character of ash-Shahrastānī's treatment of Christianity will best be appreciated by some quotations. His account begins:

> The Christians. (They are) the community (*umma*) of the Christ, Jesus, son of Mary (peace upon him). He it is who was truly sent (as prophet; *mab'ūth*) after Moses (peace upon him), and who was announced in the Torah. To him were (granted) manifest signs and notable evidences, such as the reviving of the dead and the curing of the blind and the leper. His very nature and innate disposition (*fiṭra*) are a perfect sign of his truthfulness; that is, his coming without previous seed and his speaking without prior teaching. For all the (other) prophets the arrival of their revelation was at (the age of) forty years, but revelation came to him when he was made to speak in the cradle, and revelation came to him when he conveyed (the divine message) at (the age of) thirty. The duration of his (prophetic) mission (*da'wa*) was three years and three months and three days.

This statement follows the Qur'ān rather than Christian tradition, but does not mention the miracle of the clay birds, perhaps because ash-Shahrastānī knew that it was not in the canonical gospels. He then explains differences between Christians about the manner of the incarnation (*tajassud*), and continues:

> They affirmed that God has three hypostases (*aqānīm*). They said that the Creator (may he be exalted) is one substance (*jawhar*), meaning by this what is self-subsistent (*al-qā'im bi-n-nafs*), not (what is characterized by) spatial location and physical magnitude; and he is one in substantiality, three in hypostaticity (*uqnūmiyya*). By the hypostases they mean the attributes (*ṣifāt*), such as existence, life and knowledge, and the father, the son and the holy spirit (*rūḥ al-qudus*). The (hypostasis of) knowledge clothed itself and was incarnated, but not the other hypostases.

A little later he criticizes Paul:

> Paul, however, disordered his affair, made himself (Peter's) partner, altered the bases of his knowledge, and mixed it with the arguments of the philosophers and the (evil) suggestions of his heart.

He then names the four evangelists, and quotes the end of Matthew's gospel and the beginning of John's. From this he passes to an account of the three main Christian sects, the Melchites (Orthodox), Nestorians and Jacobites, and has some brief remarks on minor sects. In his description of the Melchites he includes a more-or-less correct translation of the Nicene creed. I can do no better than repeat here some comments I made at the end of my translation of this whole account of Christian doctrine:

> The general impression given by ash-Shahrastānī's account of the Christian sects is that he had become fascinated by some aspects of Christian teaching and perhaps also a little puzzled; He was a very competent philosopher, and in the Christian philosopher-theologians at their best he recognized men who thought in much the same philosophical concepts as himself; and he saw that they had erected an impressive intellectual structure which had to be taken seriously, even though it contradicted Islamic doctrine at some points. . . . It was perhaps because of this study (of the sects in detail) that he gave prominence to points in Islamic teaching about Jesus which appear to place him above other prophets, and he avoided condemning the phrase "son of God", instead regarding

> it as metaphorical, and quoting verses where "sons" and "father" were used of the relation of other Christians to God.[19]

While one cannot but admire the objectivity of ash-Shahrastānī, one has also to admit that there is no evidence of his having brought about any change in the traditional Islamic perception of Christianity.

CHRISTIAN APOLOGETIC

According to the Sharī'a the punishment for apostasy from Islam is death.[20] This meant that it was to all intents impossible for Christians under Muslim rule to proclaim the gospel to Muslims. Had a Muslim become a Christian, not only would he have been in danger, but there would probably have been reprisals of some sort against the Christian community. Thus prudence demanded great caution from Christians if they engaged in religious discussions with Muslims. In the case of the conversation between Timothy and the caliph it was the caliph who was asking questions for Timothy to answer. Similarly, in the slightly earlier works of John of Damascus it is envisaged that the Muslim will raise questions, while the Christian is given advice about how to answer.

In the Greek works of John of Damascus, besides two versions of the "Discussion between a Christian and a Saracen" just referred to, an account of Islam is included among the Christian heresies.[21] John of Damascus held an administrative position under the Umayyad caliphs in Damascus, and might have been expected to know more about Islam than in fact he did. He regards the Sarakēnoi or Ishmaelites as having been led from idolatry by a false prophet, Mamed, who got some ludicrous ideas from the Old and New Testaments and from an Arian monk:

> He says there is one God, maker of everything, neither begotten nor begetting. He says that Christ is a word (*logos*) of God and a spirit of his, created and a slave, and that he was born of Mary, the sister of Moses and Aaron, without male seed. The Jews tried to kill him, but crucified his shadow, because God took him to himself because he loved him.

Next he asserts that the followers of Muḥammad are unable to prove that he is a prophet by showing prophecies foretelling him or miracles occurring through him. They call Christians "associationists" (*hetairiastai*) because they give a partner to God, and they maintain that passages of the Bible justifying Christian views have been added either by Christians or ''Hebrews''. In reply to the charge that Christians worship the cross he claims that Muslims worship the black stone in the Ka'ba. A number of other small points are mentioned but nothing of great importance. Altogether this is a somewhat inadequate account of Islam from an objective standpoint, but it may be seen as an adequate perception for people defending themselves against the considerable pressures upon them from Islamic colonialism. It may be noted that most of the matters discussed both in this account and in the ''discussion with a Saracen'' are those where Muslims are attacking Christianity.

From shortly after the time of John of Damascus there was a flood of Christian literature in Arabic, much of which was apologetic in character.[22] All that need be done here is to look at a few of the topics discussed and the arguments used. Several of the arguments in the ''discussion'' of John of Damascus are about questions connected with God's omnipotence and human free will. The Saracen wants to hold that God brings about all that happens in the world, good and evil alike, while the Christian limits God's creative activity to the first six days. One of the Christian arguments is that, if both good and evil come from God, then the thief, the adulterer and the murderer should be honoured for doing God's will, and not punished. This leads to the question of whether Christ suffered willingly, for, if he suffered by his own will (and God's), then the Jews have to be admired, it would seem. There was a brief mention of this point in Timothy's conversation with the caliph.

John of Damascus was aware that in the Qur'ān Jesus is called God's ''word'' (*kalima*) and a spirit from him,[23] and he argued that, since he was God's word, he must be uncreated and so divine. When the Saracen replies that all the words of God are uncreated, yet are not gods, John tries to distinguish between Jesus as the word or *logos* of God and the words of God in scripture (*graphē*), for which he suggests the term *rhēmata*. The matter was complicated when the Saracen introduced the phrase ''the words of the Lord'' (*logia*), and John is constrained to say this is to be understood metaphorically.[24]

John of Damascus shows no awareness that Christians are accused of worshipping three gods, and speaks of Jesus as both Word and Spirit. Timothy, however, and other Christian writers identify Word and Spirit as mentioned in the Qur'ān with the second and third hypostases of the Trinity. (The Arabic word *uqnūm* is used only for hypostasis in Trinitarian doctrine.) Timothy then went on to argue that God's Word and Spirit must be eternal, since God could never have been without a Word and Spirit. He further tried to explain how the three could be one God by comparing them with the sun (or its globe), its light and its heat, or with a man who has the attributes of being living, rational and mortal.[25] After Timothy's time Muslim theologians discussed the divine attributes at length, and Christian writers tried to make use of this by identifying the hypostases with attributes such as existence, knowledge and life.[26]

An important issue, of course, was whether Muḥammad was a prophet. John of Damascus denied this vigorously, called him a *pseudoprophētēs*, and insisted that his claims were supported neither by miracles nor by previous prophetic witnesses. Timothy, however, in a remarkable passage is prepared to admit that Muḥammad "walked in the path of the prophets", though earlier he had said there was to be no prophet after Jesus except Elijah, and, when asked if the Qur'ān was from God, had said this was not for him to decide, though adding that it was not supported by miracles.[27]

REFLECTIONS

The picture one gets from all this polemical and apologetic literature is that of two religious communities at cross purposes with one another. The Muslims were indeed the colonialists, who found in their religion a satisfactory basis for an empire. Yet the number of polemical writings they produced shows that they were somewhat uneasy about this deviant community in their midst. Proportionately there would seem to be fewer European polemical writings about Islam; but this is a matter which would profit from further investigation. Many of the European colonialist writings about Islam had the aim of getting to understand it better, in order to control it better, but Muslim scholars had no such interest in understanding the Christian faith, and their studies did not lead to any change in the traditional perception of Christianity. Only a handful of scholars like al-Masʻūdī and ash-Shahrastānī went so far as to look seriously at the Christian scriptures and other documents. Most were content to regard Christianity as a corruption of truth, which it was dangerous for a Muslim to explore.

The Christians, for their part, formed a number of separate groups under the colonialist power, and this meant that their primary concern was to defend themselves against the social and intellectual pressures to which they were exposed. It would have been imprudent of them to make serious criticisms of Islam openly, or to form a ''distorted image'' of it, such as was created in western Europe (as will be described in the next chapter). By way of exception 'Abd-al-Masīḥ al-Kindī did make some criticisms, but perhaps his book was intended chiefly for circulation among Christians.[28] I further have the impression that a man like the Catholicos Timothy was defending the intellectual structure of his Christian faith out of a kind of loyalty, and not because it was relevant to his actual living. When asked about the difference between the three hypostases, all he could say was that they were characterized by fatherhood, filiation and procession (that is, proceeding from the Father and Son). This is to be linked with what was said in the first chapter about the imposition on the whole church by the ecumenical councils of formulations suited to the philosophical outlook of the Greek-speaking Christians of the Eastern Roman Empire, but not to the Christians further east from a Semitic background.

Chapter 6

Encounters with medieval Europe

While from the first there were considerable numbers of Christians under Muslim rule, yet until the appearance of European colonialism there were virtually no Muslims under Christian rule except for limited periods, as in the Spanish kingdoms and the Crusading states. In the period up to 1500 an important, or at least novel aspect of the Muslim–Christian encounter is seen in the development of a fresh perception of Islam among western European Christians. This is linked with the Muslim presence in the Iberian peninsula for nearly eight centuries, though the linking is somewhat complex. The effect of the Crusades on mutual perceptions was relatively slight, but it will be looked at briefly since some of today's Muslims regard the Crusades as the beginning of colonialism. In the East the Christian Byzantine Empire experienced a permanent state of hostility along its frontiers with the caliphate, and it presumably also had some concern for the Orthodox or Melchite Christians under Muslim rule. This situation led to the production of polemical literature in Greek, but such literature probably had little influence on western Europeans.

ISLAMIC SPAIN OR AL-ANDALUS[1]

The Muslim conquest of the Iberian peninsula was a continuation of the conquest of North Africa, and came about in much the same way as a result of raiding expeditions. In 710, when the first Muslim reconnaissance in force was made, the whole of the peninsula, together with a province of south-east France, was under the Visigoths; but a new king, Roderick, had just come to the throne, and his rule was being disputed. When the Muslims invaded in 711 with 7,000 men, Roderick was defeated in battle and disappeared. By 716 the Muslims had occupied virtually the whole peninsula, and were also in

Narbonne in southern France. There were further raids into France, both by the west coast and by the Rhone valley, but the defeat of such a raiding expedition by Charles Martel at Tours in 732 showed that such raids into France were no longer profitable, and they soon ceased, although Narbonne was held until at least 751.

Al-Andalus was at first a province of the Umayyad caliphate of Damascus. On the fall of the Umayyads in 750 a young Umayyad prince escaped the liquidation of his family by the ʿAbbāsids, and in 756 managed to establish himself as independent ruler of Spain. The Umayyads continued to rule al-Andalus for over two and a half centuries, and the period from about 930 until 1000 is usually held to be that of their greatest glory. In 976 a boy of eleven came to the throne, and power passed into the hands of the Chamberlain (chief minister), who proved a strong ruler, as did the son who succeeded him. On the latter's death in 1008, however, a process of disintegration began. There was no longer a government controlling the whole country, although until 1031 there were Umayyad princes claiming to rule.

From 1009 until about 1091 is known as the period of the "party kings" (*reyes de taifas, mulūk aṭ-ṭawā'if*), since at times there were as many as thirty more-or-less independent rulers. This break-up of Muslim rule gave an opportunity to the Christian princes in north-west Spain, hitherto only semi-independent and paying tribute to the central Muslim government, to make themselvs fully independent and to extend the territories they controlled. Their first great success was the capture of Toledo in 1085. By this time there was a strong Berber Muslim power in north-west Africa known as the Almoravid Empire (al-Murābiṭūn), and these were invited to help the Muslims of al-Andalus, with the result that they themselves ruled most of it from 1091 to 1145. By that time the Almoravids had been replaced by another Berber Muslim Empire, the Almohads (al-Muwaḥḥidūn), who maintained a central administration in al-Andalus until 1223. With the disappearance of the Almohads the Christian Reconquista made rapid progress, and Cordova (the capital) was captured in 1236 and Seville in 1248. In 1231, however, a Muslim of Arab descent founded what became the Naṣrid kingdom of Granada, which survived until 1492.

In the Muslim forces invading the peninsula, as well as in those which arrived later, there were more Berbers than Arabs, and the Berbers sometimes felt they were badly treated. The "parties" of the period of "party-kings" were in fact the Arabs, the Berbers and the "Slavs" (Saqāliba). The latter were slaves from northern and eastern

Europe, not necessarily of Slavonic origin, of whom many had been imported in the tenth century as mercenaries and to fill posts in the civil service. There were many conversions to Islam of the native Christian inhabitants, though it is difficult to know their exact extent. As in other Islamic states the Christians and Jews had the option of becoming protected minorities, but in al-Andalus a minority normally had a secular, not a religious head, a count (*comes*, *qūmis*) appointed by the ruler. After the expansion of the Christian kingdoms in the thirteenth century the Muslims who had been left behind in some of their provinces and were known as Mudejars appear to have been more numerous than the Christians, and they now seem to have influenced the northern areas of the kingdoms, which up to this time had had less contact with Muslims.

The important point in the present context appears to be that in al-Andalus there had been an interpenetration or symbiosis of the higher Arab culture introduced by the invaders and the local Iberian culture. A much-quoted Christian writer of the ninth century complains that all the Christian young men are attracted by Arabic poetry, and are more interested in Arabic than in Latin. At the same time there are grounds for thinking that it may have been Iberian influence which led to the adoption of strophic forms in Arabic poetry. It also seems likely – though the scholars are not agreed – that Andalusian poetry had something to do with the art of the European troubadours. An impressive example of this fusion of cultures is seen in Sicily, which was entirely under Muslim rule after 902, and then was recaptured by Norman knights between 1060 and 1091. The new Christian rulers, however, adopted many of the customs of the previous Muslim rulers, so that two who ruled from 1130–54 and 1215–50 respectively, were known as "the two baptized sultans of Sicily".

Spanish historians are divided about the interpretation of the Reconquista and the subsequent grandeur of Spain. Many see this as stemming from the continuing Catholic tradition retained from Visigothic Spain. The difficulty here is that the Reconquista began from the small kingdom of the Asturias, which had not been an integral part of Visigothic Spain but rather a rebel against it. More probable appears to be the view of Americo Castro in his *Structure of Spanish History*. He sums up this view in the words: "Christian Spain 'became' – emerged into being – as she incorporated and grafted into her living process what she was compelled to by her interaction with the Moslem world."[2]

It would appear that the Reconquista began not because of religious ideas but because of a mountain people's fierce desire for independence. From the middle of the tenth century, however, the pilgrimage to Santiago of Compostela began to grow in importance, and this presumably made people aware of the religious dimension, especially after the destruction of the shrine by a Muslim army in 997. Men of Leon, Navarre and Castile came to see that they were fighting not only for their own little kingdoms, but against an enemy hostile to all Christians. As this awareness grew among Christians, so Muslims also became aware of the religious aspect of their struggle.

CHANGING PERCEPTIONS OF THE CRUSADES[3]

For the present study the central question about the Crusades is how the events themselves, and reflections on them in later centuries, affected Christian perceptions of Islam and Muslim perceptions of Christianity.

The first point which must be insisted on is that the Crusades were associated with a great upsurge of religious feeling in western Europe. There had been various movements for the reform of the Church, directed against particular abuses. A monastery was founded at Cluny in France in 910 in order to foster a stricter observance of the Benedictine monastic rule, and this was so well supported that by the eleventh century it had over two hundred daughter houses. Religious fervour also showed itself by the participation in pilgrimages of growing numbers of people. One important centre was the shrine of Santiago (Saint James) at Compostela in north-west Spain, but for those with the ability the supreme pilgrimage was that to the Holy Sepulchre in Jerusalem. Some thirty years before the First Crusade a band of seven thousand people is said to have gone from the Rhine to Jerusalem, led by an archbishop and three bishops. In 1076 Jerusalem came under the immediate rule of a Turkish emir who is said to have made things very difficult for the pilgrims, and this is one of the factors behind Pope Urban II's call for a Crusade in 1095 at the Council of Clermont in France.

Both the Pope and other senior statesmen, however, were aware of certain more mundane reasons for a Crusade. The Byzantine Emperor had recently appealed to the Pope for help, probably hoping that this would be in the shape of mercenaries. The Byzantines had suffered a serious defeat from the Muslims at Manzikert in 1071, and then had had to withdraw from much of Asia Minor. Moreover, there had been a setback in 1054 to the relations between the western and eastern halves of the Church, though apparently not a complete break, as used to be thought; and the Pope doubtless hoped to improve relations by sending some help. The eleventh century had also been a period of greater security for ordinary people in western Europe and of increased prosperity; but this meant that there were fewer openings for the younger sons of noble families and consequently much fighting between groups of nobles. A crusade would divert martial energies against a common enemy and reduce fighting between Christians. This was not unlike the pattern Muḥammad had followed with the Arabian tribes.

Pope Gregory VII (1073–85) inaugurated a change in Christian attitudes to war. Previously soldiers, even when fighting in a just cause, like the troops of William the Conqueror at Hastings in 1066, were required to do penance for the deaths they caused. Now, however, the Pope proclaimed that it was meritorious, not sinful, to fight in a just cause to promote right order in society. This may have come about as a result of the Spanish Reconquista. The historian Arnold Toynbee, writing from a wide-ranging perspective in his *Study of History*, sees the Crusades as beginning in 1018 when a band of Frankish knights and their followers went from France to Spain to help the Christians there against the Muslims.[4] For some time the pilgrimage to Santiago had been growing in popularity north of the Pyrenees, and many must have known of the devastation caused by the Muslims in 997, even though they had spared the actual relics of Saint James. There were various other expeditions from France to Spain in the eleventh century, made with the blessing of the Church because these were seen as undertaken on behalf of Christendom as a whole. It is thus not surprising that many men from France responded to the Pope's call for the First Crusade.

The armies which participated in that enterprise assembled at Constantinople in 1097, then marched south through Asia Minor, and eventually captured Jerusalem in 1099. Four Crusader states were established: the kingdom of Jerusalem, the principality of Antioch and the counties of Edessa and Tripoli. Edessa was recaptured by the Muslims in 1144, but Jerusalem held out until 1187. There are reckoned to have been eight Crusades in all, and there were other expeditions of a crusading type, some against Christian heretics in Europe; but the most solid result against the Muslims was the capture of Acre and a strip of the Palestinian coast in 1191 and their retention for a century.

For long Christians saw crusading in a kind of romantic glow. It was associated with the religious fervour of the eleventh century, and also with the Christian ideal of knightly chivalry. This is well expressed by Shakespeare in *Henry IV*, Part I, where the king sees his decision to go on crusade not merely as helping to end fighting between Englishmen, but also as a Christian duty:

Therefore, friends,
As far as the sepulchre of Christ –
Whose soldier now, under whose blessed cross
We are impressed and engag'd to fight –
Forthwith a power of English shall we levy,
Whose arms were moulded in their mothers' womb
To chase these pagans in these holy fields
Over whose acres walk'd those blessed feet,
Which fourteen hundred years ago were nailed
For our advantage on the bitter cross.
(*I Henry IV*, I.i. 18–27)

The word "crusade" has now passed into general usage for "an aggressive movement or enterprise against some public evil, or some institution or class of persons regarded as evil",[5] and it is now used by journalists for almost any kind of work for a good cause, even when little aggressive effort is expended. Many Christians, however, now see the original Crusades for the recovery of the Holy Places in a different light. It is not only the Quakers or Society of Friends who consider that no war can be justified on Christian principles. Even in the eighteenth century, however, the historians had begun to be critical of the whole idea of the Crusades. Edward Gibbon, who was a freethinker opposed to the organized Church, mercilessly described the pillage and massacre which took place when the Crusaders captured Jerusalem in 1099.[6] Even an admirer, such as the romantic novelist Sir Walter Scott, was aware of the cruelty and violence of his hero Richard the Lionheart. In his introduction to his tale of the Crusades, *The Talisman*, he writes:

The period relating more immediately to the Crusades, which I at last fixed on, was that at which the warlike character of Richard I, wild and generous, a pattern of chivalry, with all its extravagant virtues, and its no less absurd errors, was opposed to that of Saladin, in which the Christian and English monarch showed all the cruelty and violence (supposed to characterize) an Eastern (ruler); and Saladin, on the other hand, displayed the deep policy and prudence of a European sovereign, whilst each contended which should excel the other in the knightly qualities of bravery and generosity.

To the historian of the Islamic world the whole conception of the Crusade was foolhardy. The Pope and those who organized the armies can have had little idea of the conditions they would encounter, though some had presumably made the pilgrimage to Jerusalem. They had not the least idea of the extent of Muslim power. Such successes as they gained were only possible because round about the year 1100 the Muslims of Palestine and Syria, though nominally under the caliph in Baghdad, constituted several small independent states squabbling with one another, and sometimes ready to join with Christian princes against Muslim rivals. As soon as these statelets were brought under a strong Muslim leader, the fate of the Christian states was sealed.

Perhaps the best expression of a balanced contemporary Christian view of the Crusades is to be found in the words of Sir Steven Runciman at the conclusion of his three-volume history of the Crusades:

> The triumphs of the Crusade were the triumphs of faith. But faith without wisdom is a dangerous thing. By the inexorable laws of history the whole world pays for the crimes and follies of each of its citizens. In the long sequence of interaction and fusion between Orient and Occident out of which our civilization has grown, the Crusades were a tragic and destructive episode. The historian as he gazes back across the centuries at their gallant story must find his admiration overcast by sorrow at the witness that it bears to the limitations of human nature. There was so much courage and so little honour, so much devotion and so little understanding. High ideals were besmirched by cruelty and greed, enterprise and endurance by a blind and narrow self-righteousness; and the Holy War itself was nothing more than a long act of intolerance in the name of God, which is the sin against the Holy Spirit.[7]

In response to the question with which we started out about the contribution of the Crusades to Christian perceptions of Islam the answer is that they changed little. Many Christians came to appreciate the knightly generosity of a Saladin, but only a small amount of scholarly work was done. It was the scholars of France and western

Europe who created the new and more detailed image of Islam. The contacts with Muslims in the Crusading lands, however, almost certainly strengthened the desire for more information and more accurate information.

The contemporary Muslim perception of the Crusades was completely different from that of the Christians. For the great majority of Muslims the Crusades were no more than a remote frontier incident, comparable to British perceptions of events on the north-west frontier of British India in the nineteenth century. The caliph in Baghdad was informed, but showed no interest, though of course he had virtually no political power at this time. The chief controlling force in the Islamic world was the Seljūq dynasty, but their main centres were hundreds of miles east of Baghdad. If they had even heard of the Crusades, they would have regarded them as a mere variant of the kind of dispute that had been going on in this particular region for the last half century.

It was different, of course, for those Muslims directly affected, though they were accustomed to Byzantine raiding expeditions. They soon came to realize that there was a difference between the Byzantines or Rūm and the Franks or Franj, but they probably remained unaware of the religious motives and aims of the latter.

As already noted, some of the Muslim leaders were prepared to enter into alliances with Christian leaders against Muslim rivals; and since the Franks who had lived in the Crusading states for any length of time adopted local customs and dress, they would not be outwardly different from Muslim leaders. The creation of a Muslim power strong enough to defeat the Crusaders began when a man called Zengi was appointed governor of Mosul by the Seljūq sultan in 1127, and by 1144 was strong enough to recover Edessa. His son who succeeded him sent an army against Fāṭimid Egypt in 1169, and when in the same year the general died, his nephew Saladin took his place. Saladin quickly made himself master of Egypt, and in 1174 on the death of Zengi's son was himself recognized by the caliph as sultan of the whole region from Mosul to Cairo. Apart from consolidating his rule over this area, his aim became to expel the Crusaders, and in this he largely succeeded, capturing Jerusalem in 1187.

For a few years before this date Saladin made some use of the call to a *jihād* or holy war against the Christians, and he was aided in this by the stupidity of a newly arrived Christian leader who sent a fleet into the Red Sea from the Gulf of Aqaba, and in 1182 sank a Muslim pilgrim ship on its way to Mecca. This incident became widely known and aroused greater indignation in the Islamic world than the establishment of the Frankish states. Personally, however, Saladin remained on friendly terms with some Christians at least for a time. Even friendly relations of this kind, however, did little to improve the Islamic perception of Christianity.

It is worth noting that the important historian Ibn-al-Athīr (1160–1233), whose work was described in the previous chapter, was an inhabitant of Mosul and actually served for a time in Saladin's army. He records the conquest of Antioch by the Franks under the year 491 (1098), but regards this Frankish aggression as having been preceded by the conquest of Toledo in 478 (1085) and of Sicily in 484 (1091). This leads him to think of the Crusading movement as a Christian *jihād* against the Muslims, but he does not seem to see it as a concerted activity, and it is only one of a large number of themes which he follows up during this period. Even his perception of the Crusades as a *jihād* was probably not shared by the majority of Muslims in Iraq and further east.

Finally it is important to realize that some Muslims now regard the Crusades as the beginning of European colonialism. This view is not derived from past Muslim historians, but is the result of Muslims coming to the west as students and reading western historians. They have then noticed that there is a parallel of sorts between the Crusades and the colonialism they were experiencing in their homelands. Probably not many would go so far as Colonel Qadhafi of Libya and label the Napoleonic invasion of Egypt in 1798 as the Ninth Crusade and the establishment of the state of Israel with American help as the Tenth Crusade. Neither of these events, of course, was in the least like a Crusade. Some fundamentalist "Bible Christians" may indeed have welcomed the state of Israel as the fulfilment of prophecy, and seen it as a proof of the truth of the Bible and a refutation of the critics; but most Christians will see the placing of the Christian Holy Places in Jewish hands as exactly the opposite of Crusading aims.

The historically minded Christian today is not very proud of the Crusades, and might allow that there was an element of colonialism in them; but he would see no continuity or identity between the Crusading movement and the European colonialism of the last few centuries.

THE CHRISTIAN PERCEPTION OF ISLAM

While Christians living under Muslim rule like John of Damascus had to be very circumspect in their criticisms of Islam, the citizens of the Byzantine Empire had no such inhibitions. Not surprisingly, then, the picture of Islam which they produced could be described as a vicious caricature. After all, the Muslims were the great enemy who had wrested from the Empire many flourishing provinces, such as Egypt and Syria including Palestine, the original home of the Christian faith, and who remained a constant military threat on their southern and south-eastern frontiers.

The writings of the Byzantine theologians from the eighth to the thirteenth centuries have been studied in detail by Adel-Théodore Khoury, a Christian Arab who is professor at the university of Münster in Germany.[8] In these writings Islam is portrayed not just as a Christian heresy in the fashion of John of Damascus, but as a false religion tending towards idolatry. Muḥammad is a false prophet, an emissary of the devil, inspired by the "father of lies", and indeed himself the anti-Christ. Much is made, too, of what are held to be his moral lapses. The Qur'ān is a false scripture, in which Muḥammad included true material from the Old and New Testaments, but added other material from heretics such as the Manichaeans and inventions of his own. Islam is thus a harmful religion of diabolic inspiration, and the Christian theologians would clearly have liked to bring about its destruction. It should be added that Professor Khoury is himself a believer in dialogue with Islam and does not himself accept this picture, but he thinks that today's Christians should know what their spiritual ancestors have thought.

Since the Byzantines knew the Muslims as a rough foreign soldiery whom they met chiefly on the battlefield, they could be content with a caricature of their faith. The mixing of cultures in the Iberian peninsula, however, produced a different situation, especially after there were many Muslims under Christian rule. Christians living alongside Muslims and in daily contact with them saw them as reasonable people. It has been recorded, too, how when Seville was captured in 1248 the mountaineers from the north, and even the Franks who were helping them, were amazed at the grandeur, luxury, refinement and beauty of a city superior in so many ways to the towns they were familiar with. It was doubtless this perception of individual Muslims as reasonable and highly civilized people which led some Christian leaders to become interested in obtaining more accurate information about them.

It was from this intercultural milieu that the first move came towards more correct factual knowledge of Islam. This was a *Dialogue* concerning Islam, written about 1108 by Pedro de Alfonso, a Spanish Jew who had become a Christian.[9] The main impulse in this direction, however, came from Peter the Venerable, Abbot of the important monastry of Cluny from 1122 until his death in 1156. Peter was in the reforming tradition of several great predecessors as abbots of Cluny, and was deeply concerned with the purity of Benedictine observances. With such an outlook it was not surprising that, as he reflected on the Crusades: "there had grown in his mind a strong conviction that the avowed purposes and goals of the Crusade had omitted entirely what should have been the most central Christian concern, namely, the conversion of the Moslems".[10]

Between 1142 and 1143 Peter spent about a year on a journey into northern Spain, and in the course of this formed and began to carry out an elaborate project, first, to provide ignorant European Christians with trustworthy information about Islam, and second, to refute whatever in Islam Christians must regard as false. The result of this project is what is known as the Cluniac corpus, and consists of a dozen Latin works of varying length. It is also known as the Toledan collection, because part of the work was done there, Toledo having been a centre for the translation of Arabic works of science and philosophy since soon after its recapture in 1085. The corpus included a translation of the Qur'ān by Robert of Ketton.[11] Peter the Venerable himself contributed a short account of Islamic teaching (*Summa totius haeresis Saracenorum*), which avoided many of the mistaken ideas current in Europe, and a longer refutation (*Liber contra sectam sive haeresim Saracenorum*).

The work of Peter the Venerable largely set the tone for Christian writing about Islam during the next two centuries. The volume of this writing was considerable.[12] Apart from books dealing with Islam there were many incidental references, and these made slight additions to the store of genuine knowledge. Yet out of all this material, of which much was true and sound, the scholars managed to produce an image of Islam which in some ways was seriously distorted. This image seems to have been widely accepted by the time Ricoldo da Monte Croce (d.1321) wrote his *Improbatio alchorani*, also known as "Disputation against the Saracens and the Qur'ān".

Thomas Aquinas was not himself a student of Islam but he was aware of the need for combating what was false in Islamic belief and for presenting the Christian faith in a rational way. His *Summa contra*

Gentiles is in part directed against Muslims, and he also wrote a shorter work, *De rationibus fidei contra Saracenos, Graecos et Armenos*.[13] He shared Peter the Venerable's desire to convert Muslims, presumably thinking mainly of those under Christian rule in Spain. From his works, and others of about the same period, we get some idea of what had become the standard Christian perception of Islam, a perception which was to have a central place in European thinking until at least the nineteenth century. The differences between this perception and the more objective perception of today's western scholars may be brought under four heads.[14]

1 *Islam is false and a deliberate perversion of truth*. By medieval times Christian thinkers had built up an impressive edifice around their faith, such that to a western European Christian it would seem obvious that anything at variance with this was false. In the philosophical and theological system of Thomas Aquinas it was held that some of the truths of the Christian faith, such as the existence of God, could be proved by reason, whereas others depended on revelation; but the latter could at least be defended by reason, and the divine origin of such truths was supported by miracles attending those who proclaimed them. Some of what Muḥammad proclaimed was true, but he mingled this with perversions of the teachings of the Old and New Testaments, and his proclamations were not supported by miracles. Those who first accepted his teachings were said to be all persons of low intelligence, and the spread of his religion was largely due to promises of sexual delights and threats of force (as will presently be described more fully). Other writers went further than Thomas Aquinas, asserting not only that Muḥammad mixed truth with falsehood, but also that, whenever he made a true statement, he added some poison which corrupted it; the true statements could be regarded as honey mixed in to conceal the poison.
2 *Islam is a religion which spreads by violence and the sword*. In the twelfth and thirteenth centuries the Christians of western Europe had probably only the haziest of ideas of the expansion of Islam during the first century of its existence. If they even knew about it, they paid little attention to the fact that Christians in conquered lands could become protected minorities. In speaking of Islam as a religion of violence Thomas Aquinas seems to be thinking of Muḥammad's first followers as violent irrational men, who then brought others in by force. Pedro de Alfonso (d.1110) thought it

was an Islamic ordinance "to rob, to make prisoner and to kill the adversaries of God and their prophet, and to persecute and destroy them in every way". The implication of this presentation of Islam was that by contrast Christianity was a religion of peace, which won people over by persuading them of the truth of its teachings. It is strange that Christianity should have been regarded in this way as a religion of peace at a time when western Christendom was engaged in the Crusades. It can only be that most of those supporting the Crusades did not think of their aim, even in part, as the conversion of Muslims, but only as making the Holy Places safe for Christian pilgrims. Thomas Aquinas was devoted to spreading the Christian faith, but he insisted that unbelievers, even if prisoners in Christian hands, should not be forced to become Christians; yet he also held that Christians were justified in going to war in order to prevent unbelievers from hindering the Christian faith.[15]

3 *Islam is a religion of self-indulgence.* In the perception of the daily life of Muslims sexuality was thought to play a great part. It was supposed that a Muslim could have many wives, not just four (as is indeed allowed), but seven or ten or more; and it was known that in Paradise he was promised delectable female companions, the houris of the Qur'ān. One writer thought there was a verse in the Qur'ān permitting fornication, and other verses were imagined to permit or encourage sexual practices which to the Europeans were thoroughly objectionable. In actual fact, although a Muslim was permitted to have four wives and an unlimited number of slave concubines, marriage in Islam was always a strictly regulated legal contract and adultery, where adequately proved, was punishable by stoning; and thus the life of Muslims was far from being the scene of unlimited sexual licence which many medieval Europeans imagined. Various other forms of moral turpitude were supposed to characterize Muslims, such as having permission to break oaths when it suited one, and making belief in fate an excuse for omissions of duty.

4 *Muḥammad is the Anti-christ.* Since to medieval Christians it was obvious that there was much error in the Qur'ān, Muḥammad was at least to be regarded as a false prophet. Some went further than this, however, and held that, since he was not a prophet and yet had established a religion in opposition to the true religion of Christianity, he had been doing something evil, and he must therefore be a tool or agent of the Devil, in other words, the Anti-christ.

These are important aspects of the distorted image of Islam which was formed by Christian scholars in the twelfth and thirteenth centuries, and which tended to control European thinking about Islam until the nineteenth century and still influences certain strands. What is to be noted here is that, just as the Islamic perception of Christianity omitted much, so this Christian perception of Islam omitted various points. As Norman Daniel has put it:[16]

> It is also important to remember how much was left out even of the most sober mediaeval account of Muhammad's life. Although the pagan state of Medina was asserted there was never recognition of Muhammad's social legislation for Arabian society; the victory at Badr which Muhammad believed to be specially providential was not simply discounted, but ignored; acts of the Prophet – for example, the appointment of the new qiblah – which had no polemic value, were very rarely mentioned; there was no reference to the alliances and other peaceful means to unite the tribes; and the omission of all mention of Ḥudaybiyah, of the bloodless conquest of Mecca, of the final victories over paganism and the establishment of Islamic rule and religion leaves Muhammad's story ridiculously incomplete.

It is also instructive to compare the place in Christian life of this inadequate perception of Islam with the place in the life of the Muslim community of the inadequate perception of Christianity. After their conquests the Muslims had to live in lands where they were mingling with Christians to some extent; and their perception of Christianity, despite its shortcomings, enabled them to do this satisfactorily. Because it was claimed that Muḥammad was a prophet in the line of Moses and Jesus, Judaism and Christianity could not be entirely rejected; and yet at the same time there were serious discrepancies between the Qur'ān and the Jewish and Christian scriptures and also Jewish and Christian beliefs.

The situation of the Christians in western Europe, however, was different. It is possible that the proportion of Christians converted to Islam in al-Andalus was greater than that in Egypt, Syria and Iraq; but the new perception of Islam created by the Christian scholars does not seem to have been primarily intended for the benefit of Christians under Muslim rule, though it may in fact have helped them to resist conversion. It doubtless also helped Christians mixing with Muslims in the Christian kingdoms after the Reconquista, though in these conversion to Islam would have lost most of its attraction. Many of the people responsible for the new perception, such as Peter the Venerable, had no close contacts with Muslims. The form given to some of the books, namely, of discussions with a Muslim, might suggest an interest in converting Muslims, but there are few signs of missionary effort, apart from a handful of individuals, of whom many seem to have been more interested in going to Muslim lands to gain the crown of martyrdom than in making actual converts.

It would therefore seem probable that the creation of the distorted image of Islam was largely a response to the cultural superiority of the Muslims, especially those of al-Andalus. When the Muslims first crossed into Spain, the local inhabitants were greatly inferior to them in all the arts of gracious living, and the peoples north of the Pyrenees were in much the same condition. By the thirteenth century the gap between the two cultures was probably less, but had by no means been closed, though the Christians were now roughly equal to the Muslims in military technology. In support of this suggestion about a response to a superior culture it is to be noted that, where the Muslim perception of Christianity emphasized its intellectual weaknesses, the Christian perception of Islam, without neglecting the intellectual side, gave rather more weight to moral weaknesses. This meant that Christians could feel that, even if the Muslims were superior to them in various cultural matters, yet they, besides having a true and thus better religion, were in many ways morally superior to the Muslims. The Christian perception of Islam implies a corresponding perception of Christianity, leading to a deeper awareness of the identity of western European Christendom. In his book on *Orientalism* Edward Said says that one of his aims is "to show that European culture gained in strength and identity by setting itself off against the Orient as a sort of surrogate and even underground self"; and while he is thinking chiefly of the last three centuries something similar would seem to have been the case earlier.[17]

Chapter 7

The background of the modern encounter

In the modern period, and especially since the later eighteenth century, changes have taken place in the mutual perceptions of Muslims and Christians, but these changes have followed on dramatic changes in the political and economic relations of all the different peoples involved – both Islam and Christianity are now far from being monolithic. It will be helpful to look briefly at some features of this background.

THE OTTOMAN EMPIRE

The Ottoman Empire is an obvious starting point, because by its occupation of south-eastern Europe it became a renewal of aggressive Islamic colonialism. The Ottoman or Osmanli family was a small part of the great body of Turkish tribes known as Turkmens who came flooding into Anatolia or Asia Minor from the eleventh century onwards. The Ottomans were leaders in the continuous fighting against the Byzantines, especially after they moved to north-west Anatolia in the thirteenth century. Their followers gained a reputation as ghāzīs, or warriors for the faith against the Christians, and as a result of their successes what may now be called the Ottoman dynasty absorbed other smaller Turkish principalities. In 1357 they crossed the Dardanelles into the Gallipoli peninsula, and before the end of the century had conquered several provinces of the Byzantine Empire, including Greece and Bulgaria. Constantinople itself finally fell in 1453.

The early sixteenth century was a period of further rapid expansion. In 1517 Syria and Egypt were conquered from their Mameluke rulers, while after a victory in 1526 most of Hungary came under Ottoman rule, and in 1529 the Ottoman army was besieging Vienna, though unsuccessfully. By 1534 the Ottomans had a powerful navy in the Mediterranean and were engaging in war with Spain and other European powers. Algeria was already theirs, and they eventually added Tunisia to their Empire. They also expanded south-eastwards, occupying Iraq and parts of Arabia, and maintaining a fleet in the Indian Ocean.

The Ottoman élite saw this as a continuation of the expansion of Islam to embrace the whole world, and the administrative arrangements of the Empire were designed to promote further expansion. To western Europeans the Ottoman advance was a renewal of Muslim aggression, confirming the view that Islam was a religion of violence and the sword and therefore to be feared. It was not surprising that in 1542 the municipal council of Basel in Switzerland imprisoned a publisher for trying to bring out an edition of Robert of Ketton's Latin translation of the Qur'ān, being afraid that these "fables and heresies" might disturb Christians. The great reformer Martin Luther intervened, however, insisting that the publication would harm rather than benefit the Muslims, and it went ahead in 1543 along with other scholarly materials about Islam.[1]

The Ottomans remained strong for about a century and a half, but in the last quarter of the seventeenth century signs of weakness began to appear. A siege of Vienna in 1683 again failed, and the Ottomans were now faced with the Holy Alliance of Austria, Poland, Venice and the Pope, as well as the Russians. By 1699 they had suffered several defeats and in the treaty of Karlovitz had to agree to the ceding of extensive territories to Austria, Poland and Venice. They still retained much of south-eastern Europe, however, including the western and northern coasts of the Black Sea; but the nineteenth century led to further major losses, beginning with the independence of Greece in 1829 and the French occupation of Algeria in 1830. For the European powers the Empire had become "the sick man of Europe" and it was only their rivalry that prevented earlier dismemberment. After its defeat in the Balkan War of 1912–13 all that remained to the Empire of its European possessions was the region round Istanbul, extending northwards to Edirne (Adrianople) and westwards to Gallipoli. In 1922 the Turks under Mustafa Kemal abolished the Ottoman Empire and replaced it by the Turkish Republic. Of the former Asian and African provinces the Republic had been left only Anatolia.

Egypt is a special case. Muḥammad 'Alī, an Ottoman officer of Albanian extraction, who had come to Egypt with the army which drove out the French, had by 1805 made himself master of Egypt and was recognized by the Ottoman authorities in Istanbul as pasha or governor, and this position was inherited by his descendants. His modernization of the army enabled him to annex the Sudan and also for a time Syria, and he began to introduce a European type of education for the Egyptians in general. By 1882 his successors were heavily in debt to European powers as a result of military adventures and courtly extravagance, and the country's finances were under European control. When an army revolt threatened the stability of the country, the British intervened on behalf of the European creditors; and from then until 1922 the British Resident was the virtual ruler of Egypt, although it was still nominally part of the Ottoman Empire with a descendant of Muḥammad 'Alī as Khedive or head of state. In 1922 Egypt became formally independent with Fu'ād I as king.

EUROPEAN COLONIALISM

European colonialism may be said to have begun with the discovery in 1498 by Vasco da Gama, a Portuguese sailor, of the route round Africa to India and the East Indies. The Portuguese were followed by the British, the French and the Dutch. In this activity there was little thought of conquest or settlement. The main concern was trade, and in particular the Europeans wanted to get to the sources of supply of the spices, luxuries and other goods which had been coming to Europe through the Muslim lands of the eastern Mediterranean. Fighting was sometimes necessary if there was armed opposition to the traders. Gradually, however, as trade increased, political involvement became greater; and by the eighteenth century India and Malaysia were largely under British control and the East Indies or Indonesia under the Dutch. Sometimes this control was exercised through treaties with native rulers, sometimes by direct administration; but it should be noted that in India until 1834 the direct administration was not in the hands of the British government but of what had originally been a commercial enterprise, the East India Company.

The occupation of Algeria by France from 1830 onwards and its partial control of Tunisia, and the occupation of Libya by Italy in 1912, were not primarily for commercial reasons, and led immediately to forms of colonization. The mandates distributed after the 1914–18 War could also be regarded as a form of colony; but the days of pure colonialism were clearly numbered as the inhabitants of most of the "colonies" showed a growing political awareness. Some of the former colonies gained formal independence before the Second World War, and nearly all the remainder in the decade or so afterwards, also becoming members of the United Nations. They soon discovered, however, that political colonialism had been replaced by a form of economic colonialism. Because the world has become a single closely-knit economic community, the wielders of great economic power can control affairs in most parts of the world.

One of the questions prompted by reflection on these events is why the Muslims of southern Asia did not reciprocate by sending ships to Europe for trading purposes. There were Muslim merchants with commercial expertise, and there were Muslim mariners with long experience of the Indian Ocean. If some additional shipbuilding and navigational skills were required, they could almost certainly have been acquired quickly. Were the goods Europe had to offer not of sufficient interest to justify the voyage? Yet when the Europeans brought them to southern Asia they were accepted. Was there insufficient political stability, so that the merchants lacked the political backing they needed? Or was the Muslim failure to go to Europe due to some combination of such factors? Whatever the reasons, the fact remains that the trade between Europe and southern Asia was entirely in the hands of the Europeans.

Another matter was the personal attitude of the colonialists. To be ruled by foreigners is always unpleasant, but the degree of unpleasantness can be reduced or increased by the attitudes of the rulers. There are similarities between the attitudes of Muslim colonialists – thinking chiefly of Spain – and those of European colonialists. In both cases the culture of the rulers was superior, and in both cases the rulers also felt themselves superior as human beings to their subjects. The Muslims had perhaps inherited something of the old Arab pride in belonging to a noble tribe, and could base this on what they considered to be the superiority of Islam as a religion. The attitude of the European colonialists has been searchingly analysed by Edward Said in his book on *Orientalism*.[2] His remarks on orientalism as such will be considered in the next chapter, but he also presents the colonialists' attitude of superiority as shown in the speeches and writings of A.J. Balfour and Lord Cromer about 1910 dealing with British control of Egypt. They assumed British superiority without question, and on the basis of a contrasting stereotype spoke of "the Oriental" (who included the Egyptian) as having all sorts of weaknesses: incapacity for self-government; social and moral degradation; inability to think logically or to make clear statements; general inaccuracy; and so forth.

In so far as this was how a European colonial administrator felt and thought about the subjects, it must have been difficult for him to have any close friendship with them on a basis of equality. This is perhaps at the heart of the grievances of Muslims and other Asians and Africans against the colonialists. They were treated as "lesser breeds without the law" and not as beings of equal human dignity. It is of course true that the Europeans were greatly superior in the application of their science and technology to the material aspects of life, but they were seen to have confused this type of superiority with moral superiority, and so to have regarded "the Oriental" as a morally inferior being. In this the Europeans were not justified, because their development of science and technology had almost certainly led to an impoverishment of their awareness of some of the fundamental values that should be present in human relationships.

While Edward Said was laying bare the European attitudes exemplified in orientalism and particularly in the study of Islam, sensitive westerners were aware of the element of falsehood underlying such attitudes. Thomas Merton has a brilliant article entitled "Cargo Cults of the South Pacific" in which by analysing the relations between white colonial administrators and primitive South Sea islanders he finds a weakness at the heart of western civilization.[3] He wants us to use an understanding of such movements as the cargo cults to:

> help to deliver ourselves from this awful superstition of white superiority. But, instead, we feel we have the only answer, and of course we are willing to help our black brother, but the help is offered in arrogant, vain, self-complacent terms. We will only help him to be exactly like us, while at the same time making it impossible for him to be like us. So we put him in an impossible bind and then wonder why he feels anguished. All non-white people, all the underprivileged people of the world, seem to feel an enormous yearning for authentic reciprocity with the white man, symbolized by eating together, sitting down at a table together, accepting one another as sharers in the same food.

The various Muslim peoples, of course, were all at a much higher level of civilization than the participants in cargo cults, so that the gap between them and the colonialists was much less; but even so their response to colonialist attitudes was similar. This matter will be looked at again in connection with the Islamic resurgence.

NEW INTELLECTUAL MOVEMENTS IN EUROPE

It is not necessary for me in the present context to try to give an account of the intellectual life of Europe from the fifteenth century to the twentieth. It will be sufficient to call attention to some aspects that are specially relevant to the relations between the Europeans and the Muslims.

A renewal of the intellectual life of Europe is generally held to begin with the Renaissance or rebirth of learning; and this is thought of as a recovery of the European heritage of Greek and Roman learning. It has another aspect, however, which is usually overlooked, namely, that there was also a revulsion from Arabic learning and an attempt to deny how much the Europeans had learnt from the Arabs. Before the rise of Thomism the Europeans had been heavily dependent on Avicenna, perhaps because he fitted in with the platonizing strand in Christian thought. Although the knowledge of Aristotle came to Europe largely through Averroes, there was also a sense in which by assigning to Aristotle a central position they were asserting their European identity over against Islam. One stage of the process is illustrated by Dante (1265–1321). He was aware of the European debt to Arabic philosophy, and some of the ideas underlying his *Divine Comedy* may have come from Islamic sources. Yet on the whole he may be said to neglect Islam. He places Muḥammad in Hell among the sowers of discord, but says less about him than about Ulysses; and he places Avicenna and Averroes in Limbo, but along with them the "philosophical family" includes a dozen Greeks and Romans. I can do no better here than repeat what I wrote nearly twenty years ago:[4]

> A further stage of the process can be observed as the Renaissance gets under way. Now the former admiration for things Arabic is replaced by revulsion. The Italian scholar, Pica della Mirandola (1463–94), who himself was well versed in Arabic, Aramaic and Hebrew, says at the beginning of one of his works, "Leave to us in Heaven's name Pythagoras, Plato and Aristotle, and keep your Omar, your Alchabitius, your Abenzoar, your Abenragel". In the thirteenth and fourteenth centuries there had been provision for a professor of Arabic at Salamanca (as well as at Bologna, Oxford, Paris and Rome); but in 1532, when a scholar from the Low

Countries asked in Salamanca about instruction in Arabic, a distinguished Spaniard said to him, "What concern have you with this barbaric language, Arabic? It is sufficient to know Latin and Greek. In my youth I was as foolish as you and took up Hebrew and Arabic; but I have long since given up these two last and devote myself entirely to Greek. Let me advise you to do the same."

In the aftermath of the Renaissance and the Reformation there appeared new philosophical movements, among whose leaders were René Descartes (1596–1650) and John Locke (1632–1704). These rejected scholasticism, by which they meant the Christianized form of Aristotelianism; and this was doubtless because of the rigidity with which it was being taught. Although these men and their successors did not arrive at a single alternative philosophy, they may be said to have established a "universe of discourse" for the philosophers which was widely accepted. Out of this grew the movement known as the Enlightenment, which placed reason above revelation and was mainly anti-religious. In particular, the Enlightenment led in the nineteenth century to the development of new disciplines of textual, literary and historical criticism, and to a strong insistence on the importance of historical objectivity. Textual criticism gave scholars more accurate versions of the Greek and Latin classics. Then the disciplines were applied to the Christian scriptures, and reached conclusions which disturbed many Christians even though basically they did not touch the central teaching of the Christian faith but dealt with secondary matters, such as the authorship of the first five books of the Bible.

In the twentieth century criticism of the New Testament has raised more serious issues, but scholars who are also firm believers have parried the negative aspect of such criticism and used critical methods to gain a deeper understanding of their faith. It is important that Muslims should realize that the scholarly methods, about whose application to Islam they complain, have also been applied to Christianity. They have obliged Christians to abandon certain ideas formerly accepted about the history of their religion, but have not cast doubt on the central truths. On the contrary they have brought those Christians who appreciate them to a more mature understanding of Christianity.

This general intellectual movement in Europe supported many individuals engaged in scientific research of various kinds. An outstanding advance came in the middle of the nineteenth century with Charles Darwin's theory of the evolution of the human race from lower forms of life. This was at first rejected by most Christians because they saw it as an attack on the account of creation in the book of Genesis. Now all educated Christians accept the fact of evolution, and understand the account in Genesis not as a rival scientific view, but as a way of expressing important truths about the relation of God to human beings. Many Muslims have also been upset by the fact of evolution, and some have insisted that the Darwinian theory is not generally accepted by scientists; but what they have failed to realize is that what other scientists have criticized in Darwin is not the *fact* of the evolution of the human race from lower forms of life, but his theory of the *manner* in which this has come about.

In the world community of the last decade of the twentieth century there may be said to be general agreement on two points. One is that the assured results of science are to be accepted within the sphere proper to science, that is, the results on which most scientists are agreed. These results, however, are to be interpreted in a wider context beyond the sphere of science proper, namely, the sphere of what could be variously described as that of cosmology, metaphysics or theology. This means that, while many features of our earth as we know it, are due to the evolutionary process, there is, for the believer in God, behind or beyond or underlying the process, or perhaps even immanent in it, the creativity of God.

The second point of general agreement is that statements about the past must be in accordance with objective historical fact in so far as it is possible to ascertain this. In the literary sphere Christians have had to abandon the assertion that the first five books of the Bible were composed by Moses personally; it is now clear that, though the original basis came from him, the books have passed through the hands of several editors; but this change of view about their composition does not reduce the spiritual value of the books. Historical works, of course, are more than collections of objective facts. The author of such a work usually selects from a large number of available facts those which present a picture of the past as realizing certain values (or disvalues). The medieval Christian scholars selected facts about Islam in such a way as to create a distorted picture, and neglected many other contrary facts. It has also to be borne in mind that what purports to be a historical account but is not in accordance with objective facts may nevertheless be a way of presenting important truths about some aspect of reality. Thus the book of Jonah in the Bible is now held by scholars to be entirely fictitious, and yet it contains some of the most profound teaching of the Old Testament.

THE EFFECTS OF MODERN SCIENCE AND TECHNOLOGY

Once again it is not necessary to give an exhaustive account of the topic, but merely to emphasize a few important features which have affected Muslim–Christian relations.

When the Muslims conquered Spain in the early eighth century, they were far ahead of the inhabitants of western Europe in their material culture, that is, in the products of their technology; but by the end of the eighteenth century it was the Europeans who were technologically superior to the Muslims of the Ottoman Empire, not least in their military and naval technology. Moreover, the industrial revolution, which is essentially an application of scientific knowledge and technology to manufacturing processes, had begun and was to gather momentum throughout the nineteenth and twentieth centuries. One of the great discoveries was how to use steam power. This was first applied to manufacturing processes, then to railways and ships. This meant that material goods could be produced in greater quantities and more cheaply, and that travel and the transport of goods was greatly speeded up. Towards the end of the nineteenth century came the petrol engine, leading to the motor car and the aeroplane. Electricity also came to be used for all sorts of purposes.

Another area in which great advances were made was in the transmission of news, commands and other verbal messages. First came the telegraph and telephone, then the wireless telegraph and telephone, and then television. Finally we have ever more complex computers and other electronic aids to better, or at least faster, living. In the present context it is important to note how these technological advances have altered certain basic features of human society. As Bernard Lewis puts it, speaking of the Ottoman Empire in the later nineteenth century, "in a world of railways and telegraphs the old feudal structure of the Empire could not survive".[5]

Perhaps the most serious effect of all the changes is that they have put vast economic and political power in the hands of some persons. When an individual has a "business empire" consisting of several multinational companies and including newspapers and television, it is difficult for any one government to control him if he manages his affairs carefully. This is a most serious problem, with which the statesmen are only beginning to come to terms. Great political power is also possible, but this varies according to the nature and the tradition of the political system. Modern technology also requires a high degree of organization, and then considerations of profitability may lead to there being a danger that the needs of the machines will take priority over the needs of human beings, so that the workers have to lead lives in which genuine human values are sacrificed.

Greater speed and ease of transport has made it possible for vast numbers of people to come together in larger cities and conurbations. In some parts of the world this trend towards mammoth cities is frightening, as poor people from the countryside swarm into the shantytowns. It is to be hoped that the cities will eventually lose this attractive power, but, if not, there is a case for governments taking steps to make the country and the small town more pleasant. Greater mobility in a population leads to the breakdown of old family groupings, but this can in part be offset by new forms of association, often based on common interest. These vary from local political parties to clubs for the supporters of a football team or for those with a common hobby. Of great importance are trade unions, that is, the banding together of the workers in an industry to ensure that they are fairly dealt with by the management. This becomes increasingly necessary as industry becomes more highly organized, but legislation is also necessary to prevent the misuse of trade union power.

Ease of transport has also led to increasing settlement of people in foreign countries, either temporarily or permanently. In the later twentieth century this has meant that there has been a much greater mixing of the adherents of the great religions than there has ever been before. Apart from some exceptional cases, such as the inclusion of Christians and Jews in the Islamic Empire, the great religions have tended to be in almost exclusive occupation of those regions of the world in which they were predominant. Visits of adherents of other religions were usually rare and of relatively short duration, so that adherents of one religion had few contacts with adherents of another. Even in the case of the Islamic countries there were relatively few visits by non-Muslims from outside; and few Muslims travelled to Christian Europe. In the last few decades the situation has completely changed, and as a result all the great religions have to rethink the form of their relation with other religions.

One particular effect of modern technology deserves to be mentioned specially because it impinges on Muslim–Christian relations. This is the discovery, in a world becoming increasingly dependent on oil-based technology, of vast reserves of mineral oil in regions under Muslim rule. As a result Iran and some of the Arab countries have become extremely wealthy. They had to exert political pressure to wrest control of their oil from the west, but once they gained control they have shown themselves capable of dealing with the financial and commercial problems involved. Nevertheless there is a question which Muslims in particular should be thinking about, namely, why it is that with all their oil wealth they have not been able to develop industries in the same way as the Japanese. It might be that the Arab countries with oil were too small a base for industrial expansion; but there are also other factors which should be looked at. While the Arabs undoubtedly had a tradition of financial and commercial expertise, they seem to have had no experience of industrial organization. At various points, too, the tradition of Islamic self-sufficiency made them unwilling to learn from the West. I would not presume to give an answer to this question, but I think it is one Muslim Arabs should consider seriously.

In the last decade or two it has also come to be realized that uninhibited applications of technology on a large scale and in all sorts of fields are endangering all life on this planet. This does not touch the religions directly, but the problems are now so vast that they can only be solved by international action. The religions have a part to play here in formulating norms of conduct for the use of dangerous technology, and in helping each nation to make a firm resolve to act in this way.

Chapter 8

The modern encounter

We now come to look at the intellectual aspects of the relations between Muslims and Christians in the period since 1800, that is, in the period of railways and telegraphs and then of television and computers.

THE MUSLIM DESIRE FOR WESTERN TECHNOLOGY AND EDUCATION

In dealing with T.E. Lawrence's work among the Arabs Edward Said includes among its aims: "first, to stimulate the Orient (lifeless, timeless, forceless) into movement; second, to impose upon that movement an essentially Western shape".[1] This is a very one-sided statement, however; there was movement among the Arabs before Lawrence did anything to "stimulate" them, and he did not "impose" on them something they did not want, but rather showed them how to achieve something they wanted to achieve. It may be admitted that the advice Lawrence gave reflected something of his own personality, and also, though to a lesser extent, something of the wishes of the British government; but the basic fact is that the Arabs were not passive recipients, but actively wanted what Lawrence and the British had to give. This is the pattern to be met with throughout the modern encounter. There have always been Muslims who wanted modernization and westernization; but the extent of what they wanted varied, and there has often been opposition from other Muslims.

Early in the eighteenth century some Ottoman statesmen realized that their empire had become inferior to the western European powers, both militarily and in other ways. In 1734 a school for the training of army officers in European mathematics was opened under the auspices of the grand vizier, but before long it was forced to close by the opposition of the Janissaries, who feared the loss of their own power. After this not much was achieved until 1773, when a similar school was set up for the navy, which developed into a school of naval engineering. This was joined in 1793 by a school of military engineering, but both continued on a low key until after the liquidation of the Janissaries in 1826. The students at these schools had to learn French, and the result was that in course of time there was a body of Ottoman citizens able to read French books and pick up all sorts of political ideas.[2] Something similar happened in Egypt, where Muḥammad 'Alī, soon after making himself master of the country in 1805, set about creating an army on the European model, and for this had to bring in European instructors.

These statesmen responsible for the reforms in the training of army and navy officers, and likewise their successors, also realized that, if their countries were to play a part in the world of European nations, they needed large numbers of people with education of a European type to fill various civilian occupations. Despite opposition they kept working towards this goal, and by the beginning of the twentieth century there was at the centre of the Ottoman Empire and in Egypt a complete system of western education going from primary school to university, while the provinces of the Empire were moving towards this end.

The reformers who brought about these changes had to contend against vigorous opposition, especially from the corps of ulema or religious scholars which in the Ottoman Empire was highly organized in a hierarchy with several grades. At its head was the Shaykh al-Islām (Şeyh-ül-islām), who was one of the three most powerful men in the Empire. Before the reforms began the corps of ulema controlled all higher education of the traditional type, all adminstration of law in the courts and such reformulation of law as was possible. The core of the higher stages of the traditional Islamic education was jurisprudence and not, as some Christian orientalists seem to have thought, theology. At the lowest rung of the educational system were the local Qur'ān-schools, where boys learned to read and write in the course of memorizing the Qur'ān. The reformers did not try to change this traditional system, but instead set up an alternative system at all levels. By the second half of the twentieth century most young people in most Muslim countries were being educated in institutions of a mainly western type, and the traditional system had become a backwater.

In Sunnite Islam (the form of Islam "established" in Islamic countries other than Iran) the ruler has no power to make new laws. The only law is the Sharī'a, God's law. Accredited ulema have authority to make new applications of the principles of the Sharī'a if new situations arise. At most the ruler could make regulations showing how the law was to be carried out in particular cases; such a regulation is sometimes called a Qānūn. As the Ottoman Empire became more involved in trade with Europe, some of the provisions of the Sharī'a, as traditionally understood, were found unsatisfactory, and the statesmen seem to have urged the ulema to make some changes. When the ulema refused to do this, the statesmen went ahead and issued what purported to be Qānūns but were in fact new laws. The first of these was a Commercial Code promulgated in 1850, for which it was necessary to create courts other than the Sharī'a courts. This was followed by a penal code, a maritime code and another commercial code. Before long there was not merely a whole series of codes, but also a large number of courts outwith the jurisdiction of the ulema. Thus in law much the same happened as in education; the old system was left, but an alternative new system was created.

For the Muslims in British India things went rather differently. The British established European-type schools in order to train pupils for junior posts in the administration. This opportunity of education was taken up eagerly by the Hindus, but looked on with suspicion by most Muslims. The result was that the proportion of Hindus employed by the administration was much higher than the proportion of Hindus in the country as a whole. Muslim resentment at this fact was one of the factors leading to the great Indian Mutiny of 1857. After the quelling of the Mutiny the Muslims were dejected, but Sir Sayyid Ahmad Khan managed to persuade many of them that they could send their children to the British schools without danger to their faith, and that such education was in the interests of the Muslim community, which otherwise would sink to an inferior position. To further his aims he founded in 1875 the Muhammadan Anglo-Oriental College, which has developed into the University of Aligarh. He was vigorously opposed by the ulema and conservatives in India, called a heretic and an apostate and even condemned to death by the Mufti of Medina.[3]

Despite this opposition a large number of Muslims accepted British education for their children, realizing that only in this way could Muslims have the place that was their due in the India of the future. A follower of Sir Sayyid Ahmad, Ameer Ali, wrote a book which in later editions was called *The Spirit of Islam*.[4] In this he tried to show that Islam was not backward, but incorporated all the values of Victorian liberalism. He stretched history somewhat to make his points, but he enabled westernizing Muslims to feel that their religion was not inferior to Christianity.

One could fill a volume describing all the different views about westernization held by Muslims during the present century. It is convenient to use the term ''liberals'' for those who accept some degree of intellectual or educational westernization, but they vary greatly in the degree of westernization they accept. Many are concerned to maintain something distinctively Islamic. In *Islamic Fundamentalism and Modernity* (65–70) (see Chapter 3, note 26) I gave a brief account of some of the recent thinking of liberal Muslims in various countries, mentioning in particular the Algerian Mohammed Arkoun and the Pakistani Fazlur Rahman, who died recently. These two thinkers move with ease in the universe of discourse of the western intellectual outlook and accept the principles of historical and literary criticism, while professorships at Paris and Chicago gave them greater freedom to publish than thinkers in Islamic countries. Both hold that a central place must be given to a fresh study of the Qur'ān from a modern standpoint, and have indicated the lines which they think this should follow. Thus progress is being made towards the formation of a more adequate Islamic self-image for today, but there is still much work to be done.

All such moves towards westernization are vigorously opposed by the fundamentalists, and they sometimes give the impression that they want to have nothing to do with western culture. On the other hand, however, they still want to benefit from the products of western technology; and they presumably also want their countries to be able eventually to produce such goods. What they have failed to understand is that, though the manufacture of television sets and computers appears to be a purely technical matter unrelated to religion, it is only possible where there is a workforce with the openness of mind associated with the modern western outlook; and this openness of mind is something on which the ulema are clamping down.

MISSIONARIES AND THEIR PERCEPTION OF ISLAM

From its first beginnings Christianity has been a missionary religion in the sense that Christians bore witness to wonderful new truths that had been communicated to them and had changed their lives, and then invited non-Christians to believe in these. Interest in specific missionary work has varied from century to century. Among missionaries to Muslims an honoured place is given to Ramon Lull (*c*.1232–1316). Here, however, it will be sufficient to look at the upsurge of missionary activity which began about the end of the eighteenth century and which was in the first place a Protestant affair. It seems probable that it came about because of the increased Christian awareness of the non-Christian world resulting from colonialism. There was soon a plethora of organizations sending groups of missionaries into non-Christian countries, but it was by no means a unified movement.

Most Muslims resented conversions to Christianity, and some accused the missionary movement of being an arm of colonialism. This charge is at most only partially true. It probably applies to the Portuguese missions in the centuries immediately after Vasco da Gama, and later to Dutch missions in Indonesia and German and Belgian missions in Africa. On the other hand, British administrators in India and Malaysia were mostly somewhat lukewarm towards Christian missionaries, and in northern Nigeria they seem to have favoured Islam.[5] In the Muslim native states of India under the British missionary work was not permitted. In some British colonies, however, the administrators were pleased to hand over educational and medical work to the missions. Thus in the British colonies as a whole, though there was co-operation in varying degree between the colonial administrators and the missionaries, the latter were far from being mere agents of the former. Moreover, important missionary work was also done by American, Scandinavian and Swiss missions, who had no colonies to go to, but managed to get permission to operate in such places as the Ottoman Empire.

The missionaries tended to share in the European and western attitude of superiority towards the peoples to whom they went. In this matter their belief in Christian doctrine was associated, if not confused, with a belief in the superiority of European or western civilization. They hoped that many of the people to whom they went would become Christian, but they do not seem to have expected to be able to treat them as equals during the foreseeable future. They further assumed that their own intellectual and privatized form of the Christian faith would be suitable for everyone, and they did not seriously study Islam and Muslim communities in order to discover what things were lacking in Islam which Christianity was able to supply. In due course they must have become aware that Muslim communities resented conversions, but this does not seem to have helped them to realize that Islamic brotherhood and communal solidarity was a positive value.

In Muslim and partly Muslim countries the best work done by the missionaries was probably in the field of education. The western-type education they provided was something the people wanted, and was generally of high quality and free from improper attempts at the indoctrination of the children, though there may have been a few cases where there was pressure for the acceptance of Christianity. What is now the American University of Beirut was originally a missionary foundation, and has maintained high academic standards. In countries where there was no tradition of general literacy – perhaps chiefly in more primitive parts of Africa – one reason for establishing missionary schools was to ensure that local Christians would be able to read the Bible. The hospitals and medical clinics set up by the missionaries were primarily the expression of a caring concern for populations without access to the benefits of European medicine. It was also realized, of course, that efficient medical work could reduce the feelings of hostility and suspicion towards Christian missionaries present in some regions. One hears of places where it was made a condition of treatment that the patients should attend services or listen to sermons, but this was frowned on by most missionaries.

The perception of Islam with which the missionaries set out was probably that of the ordinary European of the time, namely, one in which the medieval distortions still played a large part. It would probably not be unfair to take as an example of the missionary perception of Islam a pamphlet published by the Religious Tract Society of London in about 1887. This was entitled *The Rise and Decline of Islam* (Islam and not Mohammedanism!), and was written by an enthusiastic scholarly supporter of missions, Sir William Muir (of whom more will be said later). This presentation of Islam repeats all the features mentioned earlier as characterizing the distorted medieval image, namely, the many falsehoods in its teaching, its spread by violence and the sword, its encouragement of sexual indulgence and the unsatisfactory character of Muḥammad himself. Missionaries living among Muslims must, of course, have gained further insight into the daily life of the people surrounding them, but many seem still to have thought of Islam primarily as a system of false doctrine. In the nineteenth century in those countries where it was possible, such as British India and, for a time, Iran, there were public debates between Muslims and Christians. In the course of these the protagonists came to have some knowledge of the arguments which would be used by their opponents, but many of those who took part were far from having a scholarly knowledge even of their own religion.[6]

One of the leading participants in these on the Christian side was Carl Gottlieb Pfander, who debated publicly in Iran while it was permitted, and then in British India. Several of his books were published, first in Persian and then in English translations. The chief of these is *The Mizan ul Haqq, or Balance of Truth.*[7] In three chapters he gives a simple positive presentation of the Christian faith, of which the central theme is that human beings have spiritual needs, and that Christianity meets these much better than Islam. A fourth chapter gives a critique of Islam, mainly in accordance with the current distorted perception. It seems unlikely that the public disputations did much to promote the aims of the missionaries. In general there were very few converts from Islam, in contrast to the relatively large numbers from primitive peoples in Africa.

Later missionary attitudes may be illustrated from the life of W.H. Temple Gairdner (1873–1928).[8] After some deep religious experiences in his student days he decided that he was called to be a missionary overseas. His eventual choice of Egypt as a destination was partly due to the fact that General Charles Gordon had been his great hero, and Gordon's death at the hands of the Sudanese Mahdists in 1885 came as a shock. This seems to have made him think of Islam as the great challenge to Christianity and the ''field'' in which he was called to work. Perhaps he was also unconsciously moved by various facts from the past, such as Islam's replacement of Christianity in the latter's homelands. For a time some of his friends and he himself thought that he might become a scholar-missionary, and he made a beginning with this; but in the end he allowed himself to be absorbed into the day-to-day work in Cairo of his missionary society. One wonders whether he may have felt that a kind of stalemate had been reached in the presentation of Christianity to Muslims, and that he saw no way forward.

Though the missionaries were in close contact with Muslim communities, their work does not seem to have effected any great change in the Christian perception of Islam. Perhaps they were too close to some aspects of Islam to be able to look at it from a wider perspective. Gairdner's admiration for Gordon might suggest a tinge of the colonialist attitude, but his long years of work in Cairo (from 1900 to 1928) show no evidence of political involvement of any kind.

THE EUROPEAN ORIENTALISTS

In recent decades some Muslims have accused western orientalists of being in collusion with the colonialists in trying to weaken or even destroy Islam. One expression of this can be found in a article by Abdallah Laroui.[9] After defining ''Orientalist'' as ''a foreigner – in this case a westerner – who takes Islam as the subject of his research'' he continues:

> we find in the Orientalists' works an ideological (in the crudest sense of the word) critique of Islamic culture. The result of great intellectual efforts is for the most part valueless. . . . The caste of Orientalists constitutes part of the bureaucracy and, for this reason, suffers from limitations that badly inhibit the free creation of new approaches or even the application of those that already exist.

Besides criticizing the methods of the Orientalists, he objects to their assumption that Islam is something static. He himself would like to see some reinterpretation and reformulation of Islamic faith, and concludes his article:

> It is very possible that this reformulation of faith is presently the preoccupation of some unknown person whom glory awaits. Once again we shall witness a formal verification of the proposition, ''Islam is for all times'', precisely because it is never the same Islam; the word quite simply designates a reality that is always being renewed.[10]

This conception of Islam as in constant process of renewal is of course to be welcomed.

Persons like myself who fall into the category of orientalists naturally dislike being regarded as part of the bureaucracy, but there is in fact a complex relationship between the orientalists in a wide sense (not just those concerned with Islam) and the colonialists and Foreign Offices. For much of the nineteenth century most orientalists were concerned with the study of oriental languages and of the classical periods of the great religions of the east. Little of this was of interest to colonialists. As the orientalists amassed more information about the cultures they studied, the colonialists came to realize that some of this was useful in helping them to understand the peoples they ruled. Gradually foreign affairs ministries began to employ scholars to research on topics of special interest to them, but until the

Second World War most academic orientalists remained remote from politics, though they began to take an interest in the contemporary Orient. Thus in 1932 Sir Hamilton Gibb edited a book entitled *Whither Islam?* which dealt with recent movements in North Africa, Egypt, India and Indonesia, and in 1946 delivered lectures in Chicago on *Modern Trends in Islam*.[11]

During the Second World War western governments became aware that it had become essential for them to have extensive knowledge of Asian and African languages and cultures, and after the war made arrangements for a great expansion of such studies. The large-scale abandonment of colonialism also meant that there were fewer colonial administrators with linguistic skills. The fields of the older orientalists were widened to ''area studies'' so as to comprise economics, contemporary politics and other disciplines. In this changed situation the academic orientalists retained a degree of independence, except that when it came to a scramble for funds, these were most likely to be secured by projects which coincided with governmental or commercial interests. The present position would seem to be that oriental studies in general cannot be neglected by the statesmen who frame foreign policy, so that governments may have to have their own experts, but that there are still many academic orientalists who pursue lines of research which have little relevance to contemporary politics.

The accusations against orientalists were set in a new perspective by Edward Said in his book on *Orientalism*.[12] He is specially concerned with the ''modern orientalism'' as he calls it, which began towards the end of the eighteenth century. Whether there was an older orientalism is a moot point, since the *Oxford English Dictionary* shows that the word ''orientalist'' was first used for a student of the Orient about 1780, while ''orientalism'' does not occur until 1812; the equivalent French words may have appeared a little earlier. The chief point made by Said is that modern orientalism played a leading role in creating a stereotype of ''the Oriental'' which became the basis of colonialist policy. The Oriental was one who did not know what was best for himself, was incapable of ruling himself, is gullible, abhors accuracy and so slips into untruthfulness, cannot think logically or give a clear statement of facts, easily falls into intrigue.[13] This may be summed up in the words: ''the West . . . is rational, developed, humane, superior, and the Orient . . . is aberrant, undeveloped, inferior''.[14]

It has to be admitted that this stereotype of ''the Oriental'' influenced the activities of the colonial administrators; but to what extent the orientalists were responsible for it is another matter. It is more likely that this perception of "the Oriental" was one that formed itself gradually in the minds of those in direct contact with the peoples of Asia, that is, first of all the sailors and traders, then the colonialists. Once such a perception or stereotype found a place in the popular mind of the educated European, the students of the Orient could not escape its influence, and whatever new facts were discovered would be fitted into it and tend to confirm it. Edward Said, of course, was by no means the first to be aware of the attitude of superiority among the colonialists. Many years earlier (first in 1960, I think) Wilfred Cantwell Smith had written:

> It is my observation over more than twenty years of study of the Orient, and a little now of Africa, that the fundamental flaw of Western civilization in its role in world history is arrogance, and that this has also infected the Christian Church.[15]

Edward Said tries to link up this nineteenth-century stereotype of the Orient with previous European perceptions of the Islamic world. He realizes some of the important differences, but there is one central question which he omits. How can it be that the previous European perception of the Muslim as a warrior spreading his faith by violence and the sword was transformed into a perception of the Oriental as a pusillanimous, weak and ineffectual person. It would surely be better to see the nineteenth-century perception of the Oriental as something new which became possible after the western European powers had ceased to regard the Ottoman Empire as a military threat.

Edward Said works out his thesis in great detail, but at many points his interpretations of the motives of those involved seem to be questionable. At one point he discusses a passage in Edward William Lane's *Manner and Customs of the Modern Egyptians*, in which Lane describes how he refused to marry an Egyptian wife, even in a *marriage de convenance*.[16]

> He literally abolished himself as a human subject by refusing to marry into human society. Thus he preserves his authoritative identity as a mock participant and bolsters the objectivity of his narrative. If we already knew that Lane was a non-Muslim, we now know too that in order for him to become an Orientalist – instead of an Oriental – he had to deny himself the sensual enjoyments of domestic life. . . . Only in this negative way could he retain his timeless authority as observer.

This is not convincing, for there could well have been other reasons for not wanting to marry at this point in his career. Moreover, in a third period of residence in Egypt Lane did in fact marry an Egyptian woman, though a freed slave of Greek origin; as a non-Muslim he could not have married a Muslim woman.[17]

Two further examples of this dubious or erroneous ascription of motives to writers are found in a sentence about Sir Hamilton Gibb's book *Mohammedanism: An Historical Survey* (1949). Said speaks of Gibb's "preference for the word *Mohammedanism* over *Islam*" and "his assertion that the Islamic master science is law, which early on replaced theology".[18] The suggestion that Gibb himself preferred "Mohammedanism" to "Islam" is entirely unjustified. All the evidence indicates that the title was forced upon him by the publishers, since the book was a replacement for an earlier one by D.S. Margoliouth entitled *Mohammedanism* (1911). In the first couple of pages Gibb has some remarks about Mohammedan and Mohammedanism which are best understood as a kind of apology for the title, because apart from this he never uses these terms but throughout the book he speaks only of Islam and Muslims. Moreover, in a later edition the title has been altered to *Islam*.

The further assertion that Gibb was wrong in saying that the master science of Islam was law and not theology shows Said's ignorance of Islam, since he is from a Christian Arab background. Gibb was in fact correcting the idea of earlier European students of Islam who because of religious interests gave the central place to theology. It is now generally accepted by western scholars that the core of Islamic higher education was jurisprudence, as has been explained on p. 101. It has been shown, for example, that in the medieval *madrasa* or college there was one main professor and that his chief task was to teach jurisprudence.[19]

A more fundamental point is raised by another passage. After remarking that "as this book has tried to demonstrate, Islam *has* been fundamentally misrepresented in the West" he continues:[20]

> the real issue is whether there can be a true representation of anything, or whether any and all representations, because they *are* representations, are embedded first in the language and then in the culture, institutions, and political ambience of the representer.

This seems to be suggesting that orientalists have misrepresented Islam because their statements were embedded in their own linguistic and cultural background; and this is clearly true up to a point. Yet the important question is rather the extent of the misrepresentation caused by the standpoint of the external observer. Most western scholars of Islam in the past have certainly failed to appreciate its positive religious values, but in other respects much of what they said may have been correct. The internal observer of a religion is affected by the same factors as the external observer, though in a different form. The internal observer is necessarily embedded in one particular strand of the religion, and will therefore find it difficult to obtain a balanced view of the whole. There will always be something which adherents of a religion may learn from what a well-informed external observer has to say about it. As our Scottish poet Robert Burns has put it:

O wad some pow'r the giftie gie us
To see oursels as ithers see us.

Once a misrepresentation or distorted image has become firmly rooted in the general outlook of a whole cultural community, it is difficult to change it. New generations of scholars are taught by those who accept the old perception, and when they themselves find new facts, these are still fitted into that perception. Only when the discrepancies have become serious do scholars begin to think of correcting the old perception.

In the case of Islam what scholars first noticed was the discrepancy between Islam as they found it in the Muslim writings available to them and the popular conception of Islam, largely based on fanciful and illusory ideas. In the seventeenth century, in line with the new intellectual movements in Europe, there was a revival of interest in Arabic books. One important product of this revival was a book entitled *De religione Mohammedica* by Hadrian Reland of Utrecht, published there in 1705. In this he gave an account based on Muslim sources, and criticized the fables and legends then current in Europe. He did not criticize the points of the distorted medieval perception as listed earlier, but nevertheless his book was placed on the Roman Index because it seemed to be too favourable to Islam. Despite this it was translated into Dutch, English, French, German and Spanish, and exercised considerable influence on European thinking.[21]

The desire for more accurate information about Islam may also be seen in the Latin translation of the Qur'ān by Ludovico Marracci, published at Padua in 1698. This was much more accurate than Robert of Ketton's translation, but it was accompanied by a refutation in detail of the points on which its teaching differed from the

Christian faith. Another important contribution to accurate knowledge of Islam was George Sale's English translation of the Qur'ān, published in 1734 along with a Preliminary Discourse.[22] Sale's translation has been vehemently attacked by Muslims in recent years, but on the whole without justification. Sale had a good command of Arabic, and had studied the main Muslim commentaries, especially that of al-Bayḍāwī, and his translation aimed at following these. Modern Muslim readers are perhaps put off by the fact that in his Preface and Preliminary Discourse, Sale had to introduce somewhat critical remarks by way of defending himself against the reactions of a hostile audience. Even in 1734 the Ottoman Empire was still an object of fear.

The nineteenth century saw a great increase in the volume of scholarly activity, most of it aimed at increasing the amount of accurate information about Islam available in Europe, and based on the principle of going to the Muslim sources. There were carefully edited European texts of fundamental works like the *Sīra* of Ibn-Hishām, and several scholarly lives of Muḥammad himself. One of these was by Sir William Muir (1819–1905), first published in four volumes between 1858 and 1861. For my present purpose I have used the third edition, which is a one-volume abridgement of the original with some changes suggested by further reflection.[23] Sir William was a high-ranking colonialist administrator in India, but at the same time a keen churchman and a supporter of missions. He also gained distinction as a scholar through his life of Muḥammad and a history of the early caliphate, and was Vice-Chancellor and Principal of Edinburgh University from 1885 to 1903. His acceptance of the older distorted image of Islam (as mentioned earlier) is connected with his belief that Muḥammad's character deteriorated greatly after he attained political power in Medina; in this he may have been following the principle of the Victorians that all power corrupts, and absolute power corrupts absolutely. After mature reflection, however, on the material in the sources about Muḥammad's early life he came to accept Muḥammad's sincerity and to have a certain admiration for the prophet of Mecca. It is worth quoting some of his conclusions:

> The growth in the mind of Mahomet of the conviction that he was appointed to be Prophet and Reformer is intimately connected with his belief in a special Providence embracing the spiritual as well as material world; and out of that conviction arose the

> confidence that the Almighty would crown his mission with success. While still at Mecca, there is no reason to doubt that the questionings and aspirations of his inner soul were regarded by him as proceeding directly from God. The light which gradually illuminated his mind with a knowledge of the divine unity and perfections, and of the duties and destiny of man, – light amidst gross darkness, – must have emanated from the same source; and He who in his own good pleasure had begun the work would surely carry it through to a successful ending. What was Mahomet himself but an instrument in the hand of the great Worker? Such, no doubt, were the thoughts which strengthened him, alone and unsupported, to brave for many years the taunts and persecutions of a whole people.[24]

While Muir here holds that during the Meccan period Muḥammad sincerely believed that the messages he received came from God and were not his own thinking, he mostly spoke of the Qur'ān as Muḥammad's own composition, as did all European scholars of Islam at this period. This was found offensive by Muslims because they took it to imply that the Qur'ān was not from God. In fact this was what most Europeans thought, though the preceding quotation shows that they were beginning to allow that Muḥammad had had some genuine religious experiences. Muslims also objected to the European scholars' desire to find precise sources for the form of the Qur'ānic stories about earlier prophets. For the Muslim traditionalist it was ridiculous to suggest that God as author of the Qur'ān required any sources, or could be subject to external influences. A more serious objection to the search for influences is that it distracts attention from the special unique dynamic of the Qur'ān, which is the important thing.[25]

The application to Islamic materials of modern historical criticism led European scholars to hold that many items of Muslim belief were unhistorical; but these generally concerned secondary or peripheral matters, not central to the religion. One example is the argument that the divine origin of the Qur'ān is proved by the fact that Muḥammad was illiterate and could neither read nor write. This description of Muḥammad is based on a Qur'ānic phrase which speaks of him as the *ummī* prophet and on the interpretation of *ummī* as "illiterate". European scholars have rejected this interpretation of *ummī*, and have shown convincingly that in the Qur'ān it and its plural *ummiyyūn* mean "non-Jewish" or "Gentile".[26] Actually, Muḥammad's illiteracy was never a good apologetic argument, since it did not rule out the possibility that Muḥammad could have had Jewish and Christian scriptures read to him, if necessary in translation. Thus the point about *ummī* does not weaken Muslim grounds for belief in the divine origin of the Qur'ān. Moreover, no European scholar today would want to suggest for a moment that Muḥammad had read the Bible or had had it read to him, since his ignorance of it is obvious. Indeed, the contemporary problem is rather to explain the inadequacies of the Qur'ānic perceptions of Judaism and Christianity.

Another matter of a different kind is the story of "the satanic verses" or, as with hindsight one might have called them, "the satanic intrusions". The phrase has become prominent because Salman Rushdie chose it as title for a notorious book. Few of those who read about the Rushdie affair or even of those who denounce the book probably know the original story. It is to the effect that on one occasion, as Muḥammad was sitting with pagan merchants and hoping he might have a revelation which would win them over, he began to receive a revelation with the words:

> Have you considered al-Lāt and al-'Uzzā,
> and Manāt, the third, the other?
>
> (53:19f.)

Next came two (or in some versions three) verses allowing a worshipper to ask these pagan goddesses to intercede on his behalf with Allāh, the high god. On hearing this the merchants were overjoyed, and joined Muḥammad in worship. Later, however, he realized that the second group of verses had been intruded by Satan and were not genuine.

Though this story comes from an impeccable Muslim source, Muslims from an early period have disliked it and tended to keep silent about it. They object to the implication that a prophet like Muḥammad could be deceived by Satan. Yet the Qur'ān clearly states that such a thing happens, and the story is told by aṭ-Ṭabarī in his commentary on 22:52, which runs as follows:

> Before you we sent neither messenger nor prophet
> but, when he desired,
> Satan threw (something) into his desire.
> Then God cancels what Satan throws in.

There are other possible translations for "desired" and "desire" such as "recited" and "recitation", but they do not affect the main point. It is unthinkable that any Muslim would have invented such a story, or that aṭ-Ṭabarī, who was a careful scholar, would have accepted it from a dubious source.

A more serious matter was the European criticism of the collections of Ḥadīth. These consisted of thousands of anecdotes about something Muḥammad said or did, and were used primarily as a basis for law (the Sharī'a). Six collections had a kind of canonical status and were held to contain only "sound" Ḥadīth. (In older works Ḥadīth were called the Traditions, but this term has now largely been discarded because of its ambiguity.) Notable European works in this field were volume 2 of Ignaz Goldziher's *Mohammedanische Studien*[27] and Joseph Schacht's *The Origins of Muhammadan Jurisprudence*.[28] These and other European scholars tended to the view that very few of the Ḥadīth were genuine history. Muslims naturally saw this as an attack on the whole system of Islamic law. The European view has itself been criticized by Fuat Sezgin, making use of early material not available to Goldziher and Schacht.[29] This whole question is too complex to be discussed here, but one point is worth making, namely, that the European scholars did not pay sufficient attention to the function of Ḥadīth in providing a stable basis for most of the details of Islamic law. This would seem to be one of those areas where historical objectivity becomes a secondary matter.

This consideration leads to a final remark about the orientalists. While much of what they said was true, they failed to balance their criticisms of Islam by any positive appreciation of the values and achievements of Islam as a religion. It is thus not altogether surprising that Muslims should become hostile to orientalists.

MUSLIM REACTIONS TO ORIENTALISM

Many Muslims have adopted or have been carried away by the idea that "the orientalists" were in league with the colonialists against Islam. The academic orientalists had indeed tried to show that many, mainly secondary, items of Muslim belief were false, but probably not many Muslims were aware of the details. More serious was the general attitude of the orientalists and of Europeans generally in regarding Islam as an inferior religion with many weaknesses, while also in some cases sharing in the colonialist assumption of personal superiority. There was also, of course, the general awareness among Muslims of the backwardness of their countries compared with the west. It was the belittling of Islam which Ameer Ali had attempted to counter in *The Spirit of Islam*. In similar vein the Egyptian M. Rashīd Riḍā, who published the monthly journal *Al-Manār* from 1898 to 1935, liked to emphasize the fact that the development of European science and philosophy had come about largely through what had been learnt from the Muslims in Spain and from Islamic civilization generally. For him this showed that the present backward condition of the Muslims was something temporary and was not due to any inherent inferiority. This argument also served as a justification for the acceptance by Muslims of European education, since in a sense this had originally come from Islam.[30]

Very few Muslims had any deep appreciation of the western intellectual outlook in respect of history, science and philosophy, and of those who did, most tended to be less concerned with arguing against orientalists than with showing their fellow Muslims how Islam could accept some degree of westernization and yet retain its distinctive identity. Consequently, while there were many attempts to refute what were seen as attacks on Islam, and while these may have given support to Muslims who were troubled by the apparent attacks, they were never such as to carry any weight with educated westerners, still less western scholars. One line of thought was to claim that the Qur'ān had anticipated various scientific discoveries not made until centuries later, such as: the sphericity and revolution of the earth (39:5); the fertilization of plants by the wind (15:22); the revolution of sun, moon and planets in fixed orbits (36:38f.); the aquatic origin of all living creatures (21:30); the mode of life of bees (16:69); the duality of sex in plants and other creatures (36:35). It was argued that, since these matters were not known to human beings in Muḥammad's time, they proved that the Qur'ān was of divine origin.[31] This line of thought was taken up by a retired French medical doctor, Maurice Boucaille, who produced a book purporting to show that, while there were many scientific mistakes in the Bible, the Qur'ān was ahead of the science of its time and anticipated later findings.

Among those Muslims concerned about the alleged attack on Islam there was no attempt to gain a real understanding of the western intellectual outlook and to create an Islamic "occidentalism" as a counterblast to orientalism. Instead they were content with superficial arguments against Christian and western views. Thus the heretical Ahmadiyya community claimed to have found the tomb of Jesus in Srinagar in Kashmir, and adopted the view that he had only fainted on the cross, then recovered and gone eastwards preaching. The evidence for identifying a particular tomb as that of Jesus is, needless to say, worthless.

Some Muslims found another weapon against Christianity in the so-called *Gospel of Barnabas*. The only original manuscript of this alleged gospel is in Italian, and was first heard of in Amsterdam in 1709, and then found its way to the Imperial Library in Vienna. There was said to be an early Arabic version, but no copy of this has ever turned up. The text was published by two Christian scholars in 1907 with an English translation.[32] The work is lengthy – over two hundred chapters and four hundred pages. It contains most of the material in the actual gospels, but has also many additions designed to support Islam at the expense of Christianity. It even goes so far as to make Jesus speak of Muḥammad as the Messiah. Christian scholars are agreed that it was written – perhaps in the late sixteenth century, or just possibly in the fourteenth – by a Christian convert to Islam. His knowledge of Islam was imperfect, for he has many mistakes about it, as well as all sorts of other mistakes, such as placing Nazareth on the Sea of Galilee. Thus the historical value of the book is precisely nil, as was conclusively shown in the introduction. The very fact that Christian scholars published it shows that they did not think it could damage the Christian faith in any way. They were presumably motivated by a form of historical curiosity, for, when it was discovered in the early eighteenth century, some use had been made of it by an English Deist to attack Christian orthodoxy.

After the publication of the Italian text and English translation some Muslims became interested in the book, and in 1908 an Arabic translation appeared in Cairo. This was followed by translations into other Muslim languages, Urdu, Persian and Indonesian. Many Muslims were persuaded that this book clearly demonstrated the inaccuracy or falsehood of much Christian doctrine, and for this reason the translations have been frequently reissued. Thus the book has had the unfortunate effect of confirming many Muslims in their acceptance of the inadequate perception of Christianity, and blinding them to the need to reach a more accurate perception of what millions of Christians actually believe and practise. A French translation appeared in 1977 with an introduction in which the authors, two western scholars, speculated on the possibility that the original writer had included material from Jewish–Christian sources otherwise unknown;[33] but another scholar, Jan Slomp, has shown that there are no solid grounds for such speculation.[34] What Muslims should realize is that mature Christian opinion, backed by an overwhelming weight of scholarship, is absolutely convinced that the book is a forgery, and that it does not challenge any item of Christian belief, even in secondary matters.

The publication in 1977 of a book with the title *The Myth of God Incarnate*[35] was regarded by some Muslims as evidence that Christians were abandoning their belief in the divinity of Jesus. The King Abdul-Aziz University in Jeddah sponsored a book of some forty pages in both English and Arabic with the title *About "The Myth of God Incarnate": An Impartial Survey of its Main Topics*, and written by Abdus-Samad Sharafuddin.[36] After detailed discussion of two papers by Maurice Wiles the writer concludes: "The fact which has crystallized out so far spells out that God's Incarnation in Christ is not supported by clear scriptures. For this reason it is made to remain in the realm of the so-called 'myth'." He tends to take "myth" in its negative sense as almost equivalent to falsehood (p. 10), and speaks of the doctrine as "an age-long blunder in Christian thought" (p. 1). Although the writer's general attitude is eirenic, he does not deviate from the belief that the whole truth is to be found in the Qur'ān and nowhere else. In conclusion he quotes Sura 3:199, which speaks favourably of the people of the Book, and continues:

> This verse carries a universal message of goodwill and hope to all brothers and sisters believing in True Books of faith, and irrespective of their label – Christian, Jew or Muslim. May the ranks of true believers close, and may they follow the path of amity, brotherhood and understanding, lighted by the Declaration of the Second Vatican Council on "Religious Freedom" issued in 1965.[37]

He then quotes the two opening sentences of the section on Islam in that Declaration – amusingly taking them from the introduction to the 1973 Karachi edition of *The Gospel of Barnabas*! Christians should appreciate the openness of Abdus-Samad Sharafuddin to Christian truth in the New Testament and other documents, but must also be saddened to see that he only finds what his preconceptions about Christianity make him expect to find.

The Christian who reflects on this critique of *The Myth of God Incarnate* should realize how difficult it is for a Muslim to be aware of the vast amount of thinking and writing which constitutes the living process of Christian theology, so that a single work, however eminent, is not much more than a drop in the bucket. This particular book did in fact provoke a debate, as the authors had hoped, but now that the dust has settled one wonders whether there has been any real change in the basic attitudes of Christian theologians. The book itself, despite using "myth" in its title, did not discuss the concept thoroughly, and further attention to "myth" in the subsequent debate did not exhaust the topic. Yet it would appear that this topic is one of the first that should be raised in any Muslim–Christian or other interreligious dialogue.

The simplistic arguments against the orientalists and against Christianity may be balanced by noting a criticism made of the orientalists' search for "influences" by a Muslim well-versed in the western intellectual outlook, Mohammed Arkoun:

> L'utilisation par le Coran d'éléments de notions, de rites, de croyances, de récits déjà connus dans les cultures antérieures, n'autorise pas la recherche des "influences" à la manière des philologues-historicistes. Ceux-ci ont une théorie de l'originalité littéraire ou doctrinale qui interdit pratiquement le travail de recréation à l'aide de matériaux épars puisés dans les traditions anciennes. La linguistique moderne et la sémiotique permettent de retrouver la dynamique propre à chaque texte qui recombine et réinvestit, dans ces perspectives neuves, des emprunts décontextualisés. On peut montrer, pour chaque récit, dans le Coran, comment le discours narratif initie à une nouvelle expérience du divin, tout en utilisant des noms, des thèmes, des épisodes, voire des termes provenant de textes antérieurs.[38]

THE ISLAMIC RESURGENCE

An important feature of the last two decades has been the Islamic resurgence. Though it resembles Christian renewal movements, it has also distinctive marks, and so the term "resurgence" may be retained. It is also characterized by fundamentalism, or, as I would prefer to say, traditionalism, since Islamic fundamentalism is not identical with Christian fundamentalism, which is a mainly Protestant phenomenon; "intégrisme" is the nearest French and Roman Catholic term, but means something slightly different again.

One important factor underlying the resurgence appears to have been a widespread feeling among ordinary Muslims that they were losing their Islamic identity. They saw their cities being flooded with western goods, from cars and television sets to men's and women's clothes, while many of their better-educated fellows were adopting a western style of living. Leading Muslims in public life, too, were aware of the backwardness of their countries and their inability to do many of the things western countries did; and something of this may have seeped down to ordinary people. There must also have been some memory of the arrogant superior airs of their European colonialists who for more than a century had treated Muslims as inferior to themselves and in no way their equals as human beings.

The religious aspect also contributed something. Probably not many ordinary Muslims were aware of the detailed criticisms of Islam as a religion, but many would have some idea that western Christians assumed Islam to be a false and inferior religion and rejected most of its claims. Apart from the Christian criticisms of Islam there was a strain in European thought which followed the anti-religious ideas of the Enlightenment and regarded Islam as medieval, outmoded and worthless; and some of the ulema seem to have been aware of this also, and to have been deeply hurt by such a view of what they regarded as the final and perfect religion. Thus in various ways religion was also a factor underlying the resurgence.

The fundamentalist form taken by the resurgence is to be linked with the leadership given by the ulema. These presumably shared in the ordinary people's feelings of loss of identity, and they would be even more aware of the disparagement of Islam; but in addition they were conscious of how much they as a class had suffered from the changes which occurred during the last century. Something was said in the opening section of this chapter about the development of alternative systems of education and law in the Ottoman Empire. Something similarly eventually happened in most other Islamic countries, though the ulema in these had not been so highly organized. Everywhere, however, the ulema were aware that they now had much less power than their predecessors. Where appropriate, they had tried to get the statesmen to agree that there should be a committee of ulema to check the Islamic character of proposed legislation; but the statesmen generally refused, knowing that the ulema were mostly out of touch with current problems. More and more the ulema began to claim that all would be well if Muslims returned to the ideal Islamic practice of Muḥammad's lifetime and that of the first four "rightly guided" caliphs.

While advocating this programme, the ulema also insisted that Muslims should adhere strictly to the traditional self-image as it was elaborated in medieval times. I have described that self-image at length in my book *Islamic Fundamentalism and Modernity*,[39] and will not repeat the description here. The main points are the finality and self-sufficiency of Islam, together with the conception of world-history implicit in the distinction between the sphere of Islam and the sphere of war. It was also assumed that human nature and society are static and unchanging. A corollary of the last assumption was the claim that a restoration of the ''Islamic penalties'' such as the amputation of a hand to punish theft and death for adultery would be appropriate and effective in the modern world. Some ulema have admitted that nowadays there are areas of social life which are not covered by the traditional elaborations of the Sharī'a, and that therefore fresh thinking is required, but little has so far been achieved in this direction. To the external observer it appears that the rethinking needed is of vast extent and unlikely to be accomplished in less than a generation.

In the present context the interesting aspect of what has happened in Iran since 1979 is that the Iranian ulema have gained power and been able to some extent to put their ideas into practice. The external observer gets the impression that there has been constant tension between the ulema (including mullahs and ayatollahs) and the statesmen, or perhaps one should be more precise and say, between the radical religious theorists and those responsible for keeping the country functioning as a modern state, whether statesmen, civil servants or others. Some observers have been pleasantly surprised to find that the latter group has been tolerably successful in maintaining the various organs of government and society, and has even brought about some reforms of a practical character in favour of ordinary people. It seems doubtful, however, if much has been achieved by way of rethinking the Sharī'a for modern conditions, and at times it has looked as if ordinary Muslims had taken the implementation of the Sharī'a into their own hands in dubious ways. It is probably too soon, however, to pronounce on such matters since information is scarce.

The pronouncement of the death sentence on Salman Rushdie by Imam Khomeini in February 1989 on the ground that his book *The Satanic Verses* was blasphemous caused an upsurge of Islamic feeling throughout the world. The best way to understand what has happened is to see the Rushdie affair as no more than the spark which set alight an explosive mixture already present. The mixture consisted of all the pent-up feelings underlying the resurgence especially the feeling of being looked down on by the west and not treated as equals. The impression was given that Rushdie was being attacked, at least at first, because he was British, rather than because he was an apostate Muslim. Imam Khomeini had already designated the United States as "the great Satan" and regarded Britain as its partner in hostility to Islam. The way in which the death sentence was publicized shows how little the Imam and his advisers appreciated how things happen in the modern world. The proclamation of the death sentence caught the attention of an international public and led to a phenomenal rise in the sales of the book. Had the Imam merely condemned the book as blasphemous and advised good Muslims not to read it, little more would have been heard of it. Something similar had happened a few months previously when Christian leaders condemned a film about Christ as being somewhat blasphemous and advised Christians not to see it; and little more was heard about it in the media.

A serious matter raised by the Imam's condemnation of Rushdie is just coming to the fore in the west. How does the Sharī'a prescribe that Muslims living under a non-Muslim government should conduct themselves towards that government? In medieval times the problem hardly arose. Any such Muslims were regarded as being in the sphere of war, and it was probably assumed that their condition would be only temporary. The experience of Christians was different. For three centuries they were under the rule of non-Christians; but it was clearly prescribed for them that they should in general obey those in authority: "let everyone be subject to the higher powers, for there is no power but from God; the powers that be are ordained of God".[40] When a Muslim with British citizenship encourages young Muslims to carry out the death sentence against Rushdie, he is inciting them to commit what under British law is the crime of murder. What does the Sharī'a say about this? Does it encourage Muslims to break the law of the country in which they live? Surely not. The question is a complex one, but it is important that Muslims should come to a firm decision about it so that both they and others may know where they stand.

Thomas Merton's article on "Cargo cults of the South Pacific" was briefly mentioned earlier,[41] but something more may now be said, since it makes important suggestions about Christian attitudes to non-Christians which seem to be relevant to the Christian attitude to the Islamic resurgence. The cargo cults are a religious phenomenon found mainly, though not exclusively, among Pacific islanders under colonial rule. These people saw the colonialists doing no work apparently except sitting in offices and writing on bits of paper, and then after a time a ship would arrive bringing them food and drink and all sorts of material goods – cargo. The islanders wondered why the colonialists got cargo and they did not. The tried out all sorts of schemes for getting cargo. On one occasion they decided that the flowers on the colonialists' tables had something to do with cargo and filled their houses and villages with flowers. Often they tried giving up something precious, even household goods or livestock, as an act of faith in the future.

Serious observation of the cargo movements showed that they were not just a way of getting material goods, but were about the islanders' identity and their relation to the colonialists. This was made clear by the fact that, when the time came for the arrival of cargo and nothing happened, so that this particular movement collapsed, yet another similar movement would soon spring up nearby. It thus appeared that the cargo cult had the deeper function of bringing a community together. The islanders wanted to feel that despite their obvious backwardness they were, as human beings, equal to the colonialists; and they wanted to be accepted by them as brothers who might eat at the same table. Despite professions of human equality the colonialists had never carried this out in practice. Indeed they had tended to act on the assumption that the islander was someone who would always have to be helped, and who would never be in a position to gain equality for himself.

Thomas Merton went on to apply these ideas to the relations of white Americans to black Americans and to the relations of all Americans to the Third World and especially the Vietnamese (he was writing while the Vietnam war was in progress). He compared the cargo-cult myth–dream with the American myth–dream:

> Like the South Sea native, we, too, have a myth–dream, but ours is profoundly un-Christian and even profoundly inhuman. Even when we do manage to treat the non-white peoples as humans, we still treat them as *inferior* humans. Even when we think we are being nice and fair and just, we are living and acting out a dream that makes fairness and justice impossible. . . . Our myth–dream is tied up in self-admiration over the fact that we know how to make money. We have this secret, the secret of cargo, which our inferiors do not have. Of course, we pretend we want to share our secret with everybody. We want to bring everybody else into the same affluence that we have. But we do not mean what we say. We want

> to use our inferiors for our own profit. We invest in them in such a way that the underdeveloped countries are maintained in subjection to us.[42]

Some of these ideas are relevant to Christian – Muslim relations. One aspect of the Islamic resurgence is the giving up of certain practices adopted from the west – no usury, no alcohol, no western dress for women. This should not be seen, however, as primarily anti-western or anti-Christian but primarily as pro-Muslim. In the resurgence Muslims are insisting, probably unconsciously, that they want to be treated as the equals of westerners and Christians, both humanly and religiously. The last point is difficult, since Christians think their religion is superior to others (as, of course, do Muslims also); and this matter will be examined in the next chapter. Here it may be remarked that critical attacks on Islam are only likely to strengthen fundamentalist trends. In the case of the islanders who filled their houses with flowers, the Europeans got the police to destroy the flowers because they thought it was some plot against themselves; but this only convinced the islanders that flowers had something to do with getting cargo. There is also a parallel between cargo and the promise that Muslims will experience a good life if only they go back to the ideal Islam of the earliest period. To the external observer it seems unlikely that all their problems will be solved by this method, but the renewal of the cargo cults after failure shows that the non-fulfilment of the promise will not necessarily lead to any lessening of the enthusiasm for resurgence.

A remark of Merton's about getting equality by one's own effort,[43] if applied to Islam, would suggest that in the resurgence Muslims are seeking to establish their identity by showing they are capable of gaining equality for themselves, and do not need to wait to receive it from the Christian westerner on the latter's terms. This leads someone like myself to look closely at his motives, since in *Islamic Fundamentalism and Modernity* and in the present work I may seem to be giving advice to Muslims. By way of defence I would say that I try not to act in any paternalistic way. Basically what I try to do is to call the attention of Muslims to certain facts of which I as an external observer have become aware, such as the danger that insistence on Islamic self-sufficiency may make it impossible for Muslims to associate with other sections of the human race, Christian and non-Christian, and so to make the contribution they are capable of making to the building of the world that all humanity is hoping for.

In conclusion I quote Merton's last paragraph:

> If our white Western myth–dream demands of us that we spiritually enslave others in order to "save" them, we should not be surprised when their own myth–dream demands of them that they get entirely free of us to save themselves. But both the white man's and the native's myth–dreams are only partial and inadequate expressions of the whole truth. . . . Each needs the other, to cooperate in the common enterprise of building a world adequate for the historical maturity of man.[44]

This may not exactly fit Muslim–Christian relations, but it comes close to doing so. If one substitutes "Christian" and "Muslim" for "white" and "native", it suggests possible ways into the future.

THE BEGINNINGS OF DIALOGUE

Despite the strength of fundamentalism within the resurgence there are signs within some Muslim groups of a movement towards dialogue with other religions, especially with Christians. Fundamentalists cannot enter into dialogue without compromising their belief in the superiority and finality of Islam, and this they are unwilling to do. Among those whom I have called "liberals" there is often an openness to dialogue, but many of them are primarily interested (as is only right) in rethinking aspects of the traditional self-image of Islam, and have little time to look at Muslim–Christian relations in any detail.

During the last quarter of a century there have been dozens of seminars, conferences and other group meetings in which Muslims and Christians have joined together to discuss matters of common interest in the religious field. Some of these have been extremely informal, while others have been official or semi-official. Among the latter one might mention the visit by a party from the Vatican to the University of al-Azhar in Cairo in April 1978 and Colonel Qadhafi's Seminar of Islamo–Christian Dialogue at Tripoli in February 1976, in which teams of about fifteen Muslims and Christians (the latter from the Vatican) discussed a number of matters in the presence of five hundred observers, of whom I was privileged to be one. Informal meetings, however, have probably achieved more than these official occasions.

A fairly full record of all these meetings is to be found in *Islamochristiana*, which has been published annually since 1975 by the

Pontificio Istituto di Studi Arabi in Rome. At least a dozen distinguished Muslims participate in this publication. It covers most of the subjects discussed in the present work, from bibliographies of early polemics and apologetics to reviews of recent books, and reproduces many of the papers given at meetings for dialogue. It even contains translations of articles in which fundamentalist Muslims express their deep suspicions of the whole conception of dialogue.[45] On the other hand, some of the Muslim contributors are very critical of Muslim fundamentalism. One such is Mohammed Talbi of the University of Tunis in a long review of a collection by Imam Khomeini entitled "Pour un gouvernement islamique".[46] Again in an article entitled "Émergences et problèmes dans le monde musulman contemporain (1960–85)" Mohammed Arkoun of the Sorbonne finds no true creativity in the resurgence, since the religious imagination has been used to create a new identity which is ideologically stronger but less lucid intellectually.[47] Many of the articles show how participants in dialogue, both Muslim and Christian, begin to feel their way to a deeper appreciation of their own tradition; this may be illustrated by two articles by Mohammed Talbi on Abraham – "Foi d'Abraham et foi islamique" and "La foi d'Abraham: le sens d'un non-sacrifice".[48]

For Christians it is interesting to see how a few Muslims are looking at Christianity afresh, abandoning the idea that the Bible is wholly corrupt, and trying to interpret from a Muslim standpoint some aspects of Biblical and Christian teaching. In the 1860s, long before the recent moves for dialogue, Sir Sayyid Ahmad Khan (1817–98), who was mentioned on p. 102, began to write a commentary on the Bible, and managed to cover the first eleven chapters of Genesis and the first five of Matthew.[49] In the mid-twentieth century an Egyptian writer, M. Kamel Hussein (1901–77), wrote a novel, *Qarya ẓālima* or *City of Wrong*, dealing with events in Jerusalem before and after the crucifixion of Jesus, though passing in silence over the actual crucifixion and so avoiding the question of whether Jesus died on the cross. In the words of Bishop Kenneth Cragg, who translated it into English:

> It sets out to ruminate of the collective sin of Jesus' rejection on Good Friday, which it takes as an epitome of "the sin of the world", a sin conceived in communal pride and perpetrated in the name of religious security and Divine loyalty, and reinforced by quotation from infallible scripture and by the philosophy that at any cost in evil the triumph of the good must be assured.[50]

Kamel Hussein has also written several other books which are relevant to Muslim–Christian relations. He does not agree with the doctrine of the complete corruption of the Bible, and is prepared to have some sort of *modus vivendi* with other world religions.[51]

The most important contributions towards a fresh Muslim understanding of Christianity are undoubtedly some articles by Professor Mahmoud M. Ayoub. He is a blind Lebanese Muslim (b. 1935), educated in a Christian school, who was able to maintain his Islamic identity without losing a positive attitude towards Christianity. He has probably a better understanding of the Christian faith than any other Muslim, perhaps because of his Shī'ite background, out of which came his book on *Redemptive Suffering in Islam*,[52] a subject of obvious relevance to Christian thinking. Two articles in *The Muslim World* had the general title ''Towards an Islamic Christology''.[53] The page numbers in the next few paragraphs refer to these two articles. The first presents ''An image of Jesus in early Shī'ī Muslim literature'' by giving translations of early texts found in collections of Ḥadīth. In this way Ayoub seeks to bring to the attention of Christians ''the rich and varied images of Christ in Islamic piety''. The remarkable character of this article is best shown by quotations:

> By Christology is meant not a theological formulation analogous to the Christologies of the early Church, but, rather, an understanding of the role of Christ within the divine plan of human history, of Christ the man, one of the servants of God, but also of Christ the Word of God, His spirit and exalted friend. These ideas are clearly stated in the Qur'ān and thus provide the basic framework of the image of the Christ of Muslim piety. (163)

In his conclusion he writes:

> Thus we see that like the Christ of Christian faith and hope, the Jesus of the Qur'ān and later Muslim piety is much more than a mere human being, or even simply the messenger of a Book. While the Jesus of Islam is not the Christ of Christianity, the Christ of the Gospel often speaks through the austere, human Jesus of Muslim piety. Indeed, the free spirits of Islamic mysticism found in the man Jesus not only the example of piety, love and asceticism which they sought to emulate, but also the Christ who exemplifies fulfilled humanity, a humanity illumined by the light of God. (187)

Also worthy of note are his hopes for the future:

> The final stage in the long history of Muslim–Christian relations is still in its beginnings. When it is fully realized, it will, we hope, lead to true ecumenism, an ecumenism that will accommodate Islam not as a heresy of true Christianity, but as an authentic expression of the divine and immutable truth. In this spirit of mutual recognition and appreciation, Islam may have something to teach Christians that would strengthen their own faith in the Truth, the Truth which is greater than the expression of any one religious tradition or the understanding of any single individual or community. In order to realize this ideal, Muslims must also rethink their own understanding of the true meaning of Islam as the living up to the primordial covenant between God and all human beings and the divine reaffirmation of this covenant in a variety of expressions to this religiously pluralistic world. (165)

The second article has the subtitle "The death of Jesus: reality or delusion" and is mainly concerned with the interpretations in Qur'ān-commentaries of the verse (4:157) which apparently denies the death of Jesus. Besides the early commentaries the works of some recent thinkers, both Shī'ite and Sunnite, are mentioned. Ayoub speaks with approval of Kamel Hussein's *City of Wrong* as "perhaps the first Muslim attempt to see the Cross in its true meaning . . . (as) a judgement not against any group of people but against humanity" (116). He himself argues that "the Qur'ān . . . does not deny the death of Christ. Rather, it challenges human beings who in their folly have deluded themselves into believing that they would vanquish the divine Word, Jesus Christ the Messenger of God" (116).

The final summary of his view is worth quoting in full:

> The reproach of the Jews, "for their saying: 'We have surely killed Jesus the Christ, son of Mary, the apostle of God'," with which the verse starts, is not directed at the telling of a historical lie, or at the making of a false report. It is rather, as is clear from the context, directed at human arrogance and folly, at an attitude towards God and His messenger. The words identifying Jesus are especially significant. They wished to kill Jesus, the innocent man, who is also the Christ, the Word, and God's representative among them. By identifying Christ in this context, the Qur'ān is addressing not only the people who could have killed yet another prophet, but all of humanity is told who Jesus is.

> The Qur'ān is not speaking here about a man, righteous and wronged though he may be, but about the Word of God who was sent to earth and returned to God. Thus the denial of the killing of Jesus is a denial of the power of men to vanquish and destroy the divine Word, which is forever victorious. Hence the words, "they did not kill him, nor did they crucify him", go far deeper than the events of ephemeral human history; they penetrate the heart and conscience of human beings. The claim of humanity (here exemplified in the Jewish society of Christ's earthly existence) to have this power against God can only be an illusion. "They did not slay him . . . but it seemed so to them." They only imagined doing so. (117)

In several other articles Mahmoud Ayoub, while holding to his belief in dialogue and hopes for its development, has made it his business to make Christians aware of the criticisms of Christian belief and practice expressed by Muslim thinkers of this century, from Muḥammad 'Abduh and M. Rashīd Riḍā to Sayyid Quṭb and Omar Farrukh.[54]

Finally, some mention should be made of the work of the distinguished Iranian scholar, Seyyid Hossein Nasr. Although, so far as I know, this has not yet led to any actual meetings for dialogue, it seems to open up possibilities. In 1981 he delivered the Gifford lectures in the University of Edinburgh on the subject of *Knowledge and the Sacred*;[55] and more recently he has edited a volume on *Islamic Spirituality: Foundations*.[56] While he still considers himself a Muslim, he has become closely associated with the group of thinkers round René Guénon, A.K. Coomaraswamy and Frithjof Schuon who are seeking "the revival of tradition in the West based on the exposition of authentic oriental doctrines and teachings".[57] This group sometimes gives the name of "the perennial philosophy" to their position, but it has a tendency to exclusivism, claiming that in their teaching alone is the answer to the world's problems. This to some extent inhibits dialogue, though in other respects they might seem to be ready for that. Seyyid Hossein Nasr himself accepts many ideas from Sufi teaching which have echoes in Christian mysticism, and this would be a possible route towards dialogue. In the last resort, however, it seems unlikely that the views of Seyyid Hossein Nasr and his friends will have much influence on mainstream Sunnite Islam or even on Shī'ite Islam.

Chapter 9

Towards the future

The development of science and technology has meant that the human race is moving rapidly towards a single world order. There is already a degree of political unification in the United Nations, though this organization urgently needs to be made more effective. There is also a movement towards a single world intellectual culture, but this is still far from being unified. What is happening is that the leaders of all the world's peoples are accepting the secular aspect of western intellectual culture, but beyond that aspect there is considerable diversity. Diversity in itself, of course, is not a bad thing provided it occurs within a unity. The place where this diversity is most obvious is in the field of religion, but the strength of this movement towards a unified world culture means that all the religions have to re-examine their attitudes towards this emerging unity.

RELIGIONS AND THE EMERGING WORLD CULTURE

In the closing chapter of his book on *Orientalism* Edward Said spoke of orientalism as a vast and powerful institution.[1] This is an exaggeration, at least as far as Britain is concerned, though there may be some truth in it with regard to the United States. It would be more correct, however, to see orientalism as a small part of something vast and powerful, though not exactly institutionalized, something which might be called "the general secular western intellectual outlook". Everyone who wants to be taken seriously in the west as a thinker has to work within the parameters set by this general outlook, or, to vary the metaphor, within the universe of discourse it has created. This outlook is spreading throughout the world as all countries adopt a form of education which is mainly western, and thus the emerging

world culture is bound to be dominated, at least in secular matters, by this secular western intellectual outlook.

To speak of dominance in this way should not be taken to imply that this secular western outlook is perfect and will never be changed. Describing it as secular implies the existence of complementary religious cultures, and of these something will be said presently. Apart from these, however, western intellectual culture is open to criticism, and indeed has many critics in the west. In course of time such criticisms are likely to bring about changes, but the changes will only come gradually. This western intellectual culture has now such a powerful hold on the thinking of nearly the whole world, that no external criticisms are likely to have any effect on it. Only criticisms from within have any chance of effecting changes.

One of the criticisms that can be made is that this culture is concerned only with knowledge for power, not with knowledge for living, according to the distinction made earlier.[2] This is the point at which the religious aspect of culture has to be considered, since religions are primarily concerned with knowledge for living. The only religious culture in close contact with secular western intellectual culture has been the Christian. Until about the sixteenth century the relation of European secular culture might be described as that of a marriage; then gradually there was a divorce; finally, since the beginning of the present century, there has been an uneasy cohabitation. Many Christian thinkers have come to terms with the post-Enlightenment secular intellectual culture of Europe (and now of the west as a whole), although no thinker has so far managed to express this in a form that has become widely accepted by Christians. Though Christianity is rejected by sections of western educated opinion, and by non-Christians of western outlook in secular matters, yet there is a close association between Christianity and the secular aspects of western thought, such as the acceptance of science and of the historical methodology. Thus the belief of Christians that Jesus died on the cross, which most Muslims deny, is so solidly supported by general historical methodology that no contrary argument will carry any weight unless it can throw doubt on that methodology.

What has been said so far leads up to the point that, although the emerging world culture will be dominated by the secular aspects of the western intellectual outlook, it still remains open for the adherents of the world religions to complement this by something of their own religious culture. The secular western outlook is, as it were, a framework within which they have to operate, but within that framework there is an opportunity for them to express their own experience of life. I shall presently look at the problems raised by western science and history, but first it is necessary to look at a general matter.

At the heart of many of the intellectual difficulties regarding religion which are felt at the present time by Christians and others there is a failure to understand the place in religion of myth, symbol and what I call iconic language.[3] Every religion is seeking to present the truth about the ultimate or fundamental character of human life and of the universe in which it has to be lived; but these are matters with which the human mind can deal only in an inperfect way. The realities with which the religions deal are such that the mind is unable to form adequate concepts of them. Human language deals in the first place with objects or actions or relationships which can be observed, such as: tree, cow, running, flying, to, from. There are also primary words for social relationships such as: son, mother, uncle. When people want to refer to matters for which there is no primary word, they use words in a secondary sense, as when they say a river is running. What the river does is "something like" human or animal running. We use words in a secondary sense to a very great extent, though in English this is not obvious to us because we use words from Latin or Greek roots; thus to speak of the current of a river is a more complicated way of saying that it is doing something like a man or beast running. All scholarly work is full of such a use of language in a secondary way. Science, too, is not exempt. An obvious example is the talk of waves and particles in connection with light; a light wave is only "something like" a wave of the sea, and a particle is only "something like" a small piece of solid matter.

It is thus not in the least surprising that, when religious thinkers try to give an account of the world, they use words in this secondary way. When they speak of "God", they tend to think of "something like" a human being, especially a powerful human being, a lord or a king. When they speak of God "creating" the world, they are thinking of this as "something like" the action of a human being making something, such as a potter making a pot out of clay, except that some go on to assert that God made the world out of nothing. For the religious conception of the world based on this secondary use of language the word "myth" is sometimes used, but unfortunately it has come to have two senses. In that it was applied to the world-view of primitive religion it came to have the suggestion of something that was not true. Most of the contributors to *The Myth of God Incarnate* (edited by John Hick) seem to have used "myth" in this negative way.

There is also a positive sense of "myth", however, in which it is the expression of religious truth in secondary language; and in American English, in contrast to British English, this seems to be the prevalent sense. Because of the ambiguity, however, the word "myth" is best avoided. The alternative "symbolic" has also several meanings and is best avoided. I have suggested that we might speak of an "iconic" use of language. An icon is a two-dimensional representation of a three-dimensional object, and is thus something which is known to be inadequate but yet is accepted as a representation of the reality. This makes it possible to hold that, though the language we use in speaking about divine realities is iconic, yet what we are speaking about is real.

A corollary of what has just been said is that, when we are using iconic language, what appear to be differences are not necessarily real differences. This has to be kept firmly in mind when attempting to compare religions. One religion may speak of God as "something like" a father and another of him as "something like" a mother; but are the two conceptions different? It cannot be assumed offhand that they are either contradictory or identical. It depends on the precise manner of the likeness to a father or a mother, and this has not so far been specified. Further information is required. If, however, for example, it could be shown that belief in a mother-goddess is always accompanied by sacred prostitution, this might be a reason for holding that the concepts are different and that that of God as father is superior.

It further follows from the fact that religious language is largely iconic that there can be no intellectual criterion which enables one to compare religions in respect of truth and falsehood, or even of relative truth and falsehood. There is a criterion which may be applied, but it is the practical criterion of "fruits" (which will be discussed more fully in the next section). The fruits consist of the quality of life achieved by those who live according to a particular system of religious belief, that is, a particular representation of the character of the universe and of human life. If the quality of life is in general good, then it can be said that the system of belief is more or less true. Because the language used is iconic, and so only tells people that the realities are something like what is stated, it is difficult to speak of absolute truth, but one could say that, as a guide to living, the system of belief is completely satisfactory. In a theoretical discussion such as the present it is necessary to look at such subtleties, but in the actual business of living it is best to forget them and to accept the iconic terms naïvely at their face value. For the intellectual person this might be described as adopting an attitude of sophisticated naïvety.

After this consideration of the nature of religious language we may turn to the emerging world culture and to the two aspects most relevant to religion of its secular intellectual outlook, namely, the acceptance of the assured results of science and the acceptance of modern historical methodology. For the believer in God it is important to insist that the assured results of science are only to be accepted within the sphere proper to science. As Aristotle recognized when he entitled a book *Meta ta phusika*, there is a sphere beyond science. The term "metaphysics" has gone out of fashion, but the sphere beyond science is still there, and is what the believer in God is concerned with when he speaks of God as creator. To say that God created the universe or cosmic process and that he controls it may be seen not so much as an assertion about some vague metaphysical realm, but rather as an assertion about the character of the cosmic process, about the end towards which it is moving and about how it is directed towards this end. These are matters which cannot be dealt with by the experimental methods of science, though they can in a sense be verified by the criterion of fruits.

The difficulties caused for Christians by Charles Darwin's *Origin of Species* can be seen as due to the fact that they were understanding the first chapter of Genesis as making scientific statements. Later Christian thinkers have come to realize that the assertion that God created the universe belongs to the sphere beyond science, and can neither be refuted nor confirmed by any statement made by scientists within their proper sphere. Many Muslims have not yet come to terms with the fact of evolution. The First World Conference of Muslim Education (1977), to which I have referred elsewhere,[4] complained that the basic assumptions behind the sciences were not taken from religion and hoped that Muslim scholars could produce Islamic concepts to replace these. Evolution was probably one of the things they had in mind when they spoke in this way, but their solution was misconceived. The religious scholar cannot produce concepts for scientists to use within the sphere of science, but what he can do is to provide a more comprehensive view of the cosmic process as created by God within which the scientists can operate freely.

The other point where believers in God have to accept the secular western outlook is in historical methodology. This is a more complex matter than the acceptance of scientific results. A work of history is not simply the presentation of a set of objective historical facts, because the facts presented have been selected in relation to certain values. The historian writes from a specific perspective, of which these values are a part. This is the sort of thing Edward Said was emphasizing when he said orientalists were misrepresenting Islam because they were embedded in their own language, culture and political ambience; that is, they had a perspective largely determined by the milieu in which they lived. Clearly, when two people view the same facts from different perspectives, they will see them differently. What is important here is that, whatever the perspective, objective facts which are generally accepted by historians as such, must not be denied. There is, of course, a certain latitude for the historian in the precise form in which he presents a fact; when the same human action is looked at from different perspectives, it may be attributed to different motives. In this way objective fact can merge into interpretation. The essential point, however, is that, where objective fact has been established by sound historical methods, it must be accepted; e.g. the meaning of the Qur'ānic *ummī* as "gentile" or "non-Jewish".

It has further to be noted, however, that there is also what might be called a "mythic" use of quasi-historical fact. The book of Jonah in the Bible was cited as an example of this. A "myth" in the positive sense is often a story which is presented as something historical, although it has no basis, or at least no secure basis, in objective historical fact. An example would be the story of Adam and Eve in the book of Genesis. This has no place in a scientific account of the origins of the human race, but in Jewish and Christian thinking it has become the vehicle of important truths about humanity in its relation to God and about human brotherhood. Science within its proper sphere cannot give an alternative account of human beginnings which will enshrine these values; but the religious thinker must not interpret the story in such a way as to infringe the province of science, for example, to claim that it answers the scientific question whether the human race evolved from pre-human life at one point or several.

Every genuine community lives by myths in this positive sense. In the article on cargo cults, Thomas Merton mentioned some of the myths by which the United States lives, such as the myth of white supremacy and the myth that Americans are utterly scientific and rational. Then he went on to suggest that this latter was one of their chief myths and that their lives were "embedded in an enormous amount of mythology" which was not unlike that of the islanders, only more complex and sophisticated.[5] Here, while accepting the positive idea of myth as that by which a community lives, he criticizes much American mythology as bad or inadequate. When he goes on to speak of the American "myth–dream" he seems to mean an inadequate myth which cannot deliver the results it promises.

This conception of the myth as the basis of a community is used by the Muslim thinker, Mohammed Arkoun, when speaking about the Umma or ideal Islamic community. If I understand him correctly, he holds that the myth of the ideal Umma, based on the experiences of the early inaugurative period, provides the dynamic for Muslim activity today, but is not to be confused with objective (concrete) historical fact, or made an ideology:

> L'Umma idéale ne peut avoir d'existence historique sans ces postulats constitutifs d'une conscience mythique. Celle-ci a une efficacité et une traduction historiques qui rejaillissent sur la représentation de l'Âge inaugurateur. Voilà pourquoi tout le discours islamique actuel s'évertue à imposer la validité "historique" du Modèle légué par l'Âge inaugurateur. En refusant de reconnaître la fonction spécifique du mythe qui dynamise la conscience des acteurs, mais ne se confond pas avec les productions historiques concrètes de cette conscience, les militants islamistes s'éloignent à la fois de l'Âge inaugurateur dont ils veulent s'inspirer et des forces positives de l'action historique.[6]

I have elsewhere spoken of the Islamic self-image as maintained by the fundamentalists, and this would seem to be similar to what Mohammed Arkoun meant by "conscience mythique" or at least to part of that, though it may be verging on ideology. The use in English of "myth" in this sense is not altogether satisfactory. Stories which are not in accordance with historical fact could be described as presenting truth in iconic form, since the believer in accepting a story as expressing important realities knows that it is not objective fact at the superficial level.

The word "picture" is another possibility here, or, if something more precise is required, a compound such as "history-picture" could be used. The Christian could then say that the story of the Wise Men (Magi) bringing gifts to the baby Jesus at Bethlehem, though almost certainly without any objective basis, is an important part of the Christian history-picture and to be accepted as such. One would hope that Muslims would accept a similar account of the reference in the Qur'ān to Abraham and Ishmael at Mecca, since, although it is virtually certain that Abraham never reached Mecca, this is a history-picture expressing an important truth about the relation of Islam to the Abrahamic tradition.

Acceptance of modern historical methodology also raises serious questions for Muslims about the Qur'ān, though not so much about the Qur'ān itself as about their theories regarding the nature of revelation. History shows that there are mistakes of fact in the Qur'ān, of which the most serious is its inadequate perception of Christianity (as described in Chapter 2). If Muslims maintain that the Qur'ān is the pure unadulterated speech of God without the admixture of anything human, then it is impossible to explain errors of this kind – unless one is prepared to say that God was deceiving the Muslims, which God forbid. The Qur'ān itself does not support such a theory of the nature of revelation, since it claims to be an Arabic Qur'ān, and Arabic is a human language. A language, too, is closely associated with the whole experience of living of those who speak it, especially the forms of social, economic and political relationships they have found satisfactory; and these forms are different from those of other peoples, as was noted above.[7] It is also widely agreed by believers in God that his revelations are directed primarily to the needs of the groups towards whom they are addressed; but it is not agreed how the adaptation to a particular human situation comes about. Is it not possible that in the course of the adaptation errors came in, and yet not in such a way as to alter the central truths of the revelation. What other believers in God would hope for would be that Muslims would find a way of maintaining the general truth of the Qur'ān, but without denying that in some secondary matters there were slight errors.

The question to which all these considerations are leading is whether Muslims want to share in the life of the "one world" into which we are moving, or whether, because they regard Islam as self-sufficient, they want to remain in isolation until they have converted the rest of the world. If they want to share, then they must accept the secular aspects of the emerging world culture, and try to show others how the religious values of Islam complement that secular culture. They cannot do this, however, if they remain content, as the fundamentalists do, with the expression of Islam in terms of twelfth-century science and philosophy.

If Muslims are prepared to take a full share in the political life of the one world, even in the imperfect form of the present United Nations, there is much which they have to contribute. It is widely held that Islam has been more successful than Christianity in bringing religious and moral values to bear on political life. There is obviously much to be done in formulating a political morality for the twenty-first century so that a measure of control can be exercised over individuals and groups who wield vast power, either economically or politically. To this Muslims have an important contribution to make.

LIVING WITH OTHER RELIGIONS

It would seem to be the case that the adherents of each religion consider it to be superior to all others. Some adherents of religions, notably some Christians and Muslims, think that their religion is the only religion in the proper sense, and that all the others are something less; they give as grounds for this such assertions as that "my religion alone is from God, and the others are no more than human inventions" or "my religion alone has divine truth in its purity, while all the others have somehow corrupted it". These exclusivist views cannot be held within the emerging world culture, because social science is part of the western intellectual outlook, and social-scientific observation of religions shows that they are all doing more or less the same things, with similar aims and with a measure of success. John Hick makes this point about similarity very forcibly by quoting Jewish, Muslim, Sikh and Hindu prayers which are hardly different from Christian prayers.[8] Even if the believer only claims that his religion is superior to others, it is still difficult for him to meet adherents of other religions as equals. How can this come about?

It has already been maintained that, because the intellectual content of religious belief is expressed in iconic terms, there can be no intellectual criterion of the truth of beliefs, and that doctrines which seem to be contradictory may not in fact be contradictory but perhaps complementary. If this point is accepted there can be no rational justification for asserting publicly that one's religion is better than others (even if one goes on thinking that it is), and thus at least a partial justification for accepting other religions as equals.

The criterion of "fruits" as applying to religions has already been mentioned, and indeed should have a central place in Christian thinking, since it comes from the Sermon on the Mount; there Jesus said that religious teachers are to be judged according to the quality of the fruit of their teaching, in the same way that a good tree is distinguished from an inferior one by the quality of its fruit.[9] If this conception is applied to religion, then one can say that a religion produces good fruit when it enables the majority of its members to

lead meaningful lives in a harmonious community, despite the existence of pain and suffering. This is clearly not a criterion that can be applied with mathematical rigour, but there could be a wide area of agreement between people from different traditions as to what constitutes good fruit. One point to be noticed, however, is that the subjective feeling of being satisfied with one's religion is not in itself sufficient. It is unfortunately the case that there are some forms of Christianity, and probably of other religions too, where satisfaction with one's religion has become a form of self-complacency which is blind to injustice in one's surroundings, injustice from which the complacent individuals may even be profiting.

Once the criterion of fruits has been accepted, it would be reasonable to hold that all the great religions and most of the lesser ones have produced good fruits for most of their adherents. When one sees a poor Indian cripple boy begging with a serenely happy smile on his face, one is bound to acknowledge that a religion which achieves this for him is worthy of admiration. It may further be argued that, if a religion has good fruits, then its picture of the universe and of the place of human life in it must be true, at least up to the point of being adequate guidance for its members in the business of living. Because the picture is expressed in iconic language or history-pictures, it may be better to speak of adequacy than of truth. That the religions have good fruits becomes a further reason for accepting them as equal to one's own in principle. It is not feasible to assign degrees of adequacy to the various religions.

In connection with the criterion of fruits it is also important to notice that through several centuries what is regarded as the same religion may have different fruits from century to century. This is because a religion is a living, growing, changing thing, even when it makes no change in its scriptural and doctrinal basis. After the wars of religion in the sixteenth and seventeenth centuries, European Christianity, in both Catholic and Protestant forms, tended to become a purely personal matter, something privatized, and to make no pronouncements on public policy; there was here no change of creed but only of emphasis. In the time of John the Baptist and Jesus there were different groups within the Jewish religion, who practised it in different ways. The Sadducees compromised with the Roman colonialists; the Zealots thought only of a military solution; the Pharisees placed undue emphasis on ritual purity at the expense of moral virtues. This last was perhaps only one strand within Pharisaism, since the renewal of Jewish religion after the fall of Jerusalem in AD 70 was largely due to the Pharisees; but there must have been many Pharisees who had altered their religion by placing undue emphasis on ritual purity in forms which it was impossible for ordinary Jews to observe.

It may further be argued that the existence of fruits in the religions shows that God has been working in all of them. This statement is made in the theistic form suited to the three Abrahamic religions, but an equivalent statement could presumably be made in non-theistic, say Buddhist, terms. It has been suggested by some Christian theologians that, since God is always the same, the diversity in the religions has come about through the human response to God; but this seems to simplify the matter unduly. God was never apprehended as he is in himself, but only as people saw something of his activity and his mystery within the life of their own culture. That means that when they came to understand something of God, they spoke of it in terms of their own culture, that is, in their own language and own categories of thought; and this would be true even of the messages from beyond themselves received by prophets. Moreover what each culture saw of God, or had revealed to them by God, would also depend on their own experience of the problems of living, and these may have varied from culture to culture (as was indicated in the first chapter). In this way it comes about that some religions, such as most forms of Buddhism, do not speak about God. Since this book is about Islam and Christianity chiefly, it will be convenient to speak about God and not to try to bring in the non-theistic religions.

The idea that God has revealed himself in some manner to all men is found at various points in the Bible, and first of all in his covenant with Noah.[10] At the end of the Old Testament the prophet Malachi speaks of God's name being great among the Gentiles from the rising of the sun to its going down, and incense being offered to him.[11] In the New Testament, too, Jesus says that many will come from east and west (that is, non-Jews) and will sit down with Abraham, Isaac and Jacob in the banquet in the kingdom of heaven.[12] In Islam, too, the Qur'ān implies that all peoples have received some knowledge of God.[13] In accordance with this line of thinking we could now give a version of world religious history.

About the year 1800 BC God revealed to a man called Abraham some knowledge of himself, of his purposes for the human race, and of the forms of conduct he expected from human beings. In a sense God chose Abraham, though not to place him above other human beings, but so that he could be a channel through which this aspect of the knowledge of God could come to all the families of the earth.

Abraham's knowledge and practice were preserved among his descendants even after they had spent over four hundred years in Egypt; and about 1250 BC God inspired Moses to lead the Israelites out of Egypt and to give them a fuller understanding of God's control of worldly events and of his laws for humanity. The Israelites managed to settle in Palestine, and about the year 1000 BC became a united people under King David. In the period of four or five centuries after about 900 BC great religious leaders appeared in various parts of the world: Confucius in China, the Buddha in India, Zoroaster in Persia and many others. Perhaps one might also add Socrates, Plato and Pythagoras in Greece. All these brought new and deeper religious insights to the peoples among whom they lived.

After King David the Israelites had some ups and downs, but when they deviated from the true faith, they were recalled to it by a series of prophets. The prophets also brought fresh and fuller understanding of God and of his activities in the world. On this basis the Israelites were able to recover from the catastrophic experience of the Exile to Iraq (in 586), and to rebuild a believing community after their restoration of Jerusalem. By the time of John the Baptist and Jesus emphases had entered into some strands of the Jewish religion which impaired the purity of the Jews' witness to God before the non-Jewish world, and even threatened their ability to continue any witness. It was to correct this deviation that God sent first John the Baptist and then Jesus to the Jewish people.

It is difficult for Christians to give an account of Jesus suitable for inclusion in a version of religious world-history in which all religions are treated as being on an equal footing. Such an account must not be exclusivist. I suggest that this is to be done by presenting the teaching and achievement of Jesus solely in terms of historical human fact and without the theological interpretations of early and later Christians. This appears to be theologically sound, since the first disciples came to know Jesus as a human being before they came to think that he must be in some sense divine. This method was tried out by a pioneering missionary to the primitive Masai tribe in Kenya, and found successful; and he justified what he had done by pointing to the experience of the disciples:

> There was no other way for the disciples of Jesus to come to know him, except through the human life he lived among them. No other way to come to the deepest meaning of what lay within, except by reflection on what was clearly visible and audible and sensible and

touchable without. And there is no other way for the Masai of today to come to the fullest meaning of what happened back there in Galilee long ago.[14]

This would also appear to be the way to present the Christian faith to non-Christians in this religiously pluralistic world, namely, to give them the historical human facts about Jesus and then to allow them to interpret these facts in terms of their own religious values.

The work of John the Baptist and Jesus as teachers was to correct some of the false emphases in contemporary Jewish attitudes, such as strongly asserting God's love for the repentant sinner. Apart from teaching, however, Jesus also achieved something of importance for the world through his death and what followed it. This achievement has been described by Christians in various ways, such as the redemption of the world, the bringing of salvation, the reconciling of humanity with God, the inauguration of a new covenant between God and the whole human race. All these phrases, and others also used, are iconic, so that none is a perfect expression of the whole truth, while some include a degree of interpretation leading to exclusivism. For the purposes of our version of world religious history it would perhaps be best to say that the achievement by his death was to inaugurate a new covenant or form of relationship between God and the human race, in which the emphasis was on God's love for all. As the disciples of Jesus and other early Christians came to understand this achievement and to interpret it theologically, the Church was established; and then it grew until in the fourth century it became the official religion of the Roman Empire.

Meanwhile the religions of southern and eastern Asia were growing and developing. Christianity also spread eastwards, but, as explained in Chapter 1, a rift developed between the Greek or Hellenized Christians of the Roman or Byzantine Empire and the Semitic and less Hellenized Christians on their eastern borders. In this situation, however it is understood in detail, there was scope for a new divine initiative in human affairs, and this came about through Muḥammad. The rapid expansion of Islam may be attributed, partly to its inherently Abrahamic character, and partly to the weaknesses in some forms of Christianity. During the following centuries, apart from the encounters between Muslims and Christians described in previous chapters, and the special case of the Jews, each of the great religions remained largely isolated from the others. It is only in the twentieth century that large-scale movements of population have taken place which are forcing the religions to take cognizance of the problems of religious pluralism, the problems of religions living together.

The main solutions to these contemporary problems fall under the headings of mission and dialogue; is each religion to try to convert the others, or are they to engage in dialogue? There is a third possibility, trying to remain in isolation, and there are strands in Islam, and perhaps other religions, which favour this; but separate existence is not viable in today's world unless one is content to shut oneself up in a ghetto. Both Christianity and Islam engage in mission, though many Muslims try to maintain that what they do is different from what Christians do. In Arabic the missionary work of Christians is usually *tabshīr*, evangelization or spreading the good news, but with objectionable connotations, whereas Islamic mission is *da'wa*, calling or summoning to *islām*, to submission to God; and "The Islamic Call Society" is the name Colonel Qadhafi gives to the missionary association he supports.

To understand this alleged distinction it is helpful to consider what is involved in conversion from one religious group to another religious group. In such conversions there are two types of factors, communal factors and personal factors. In the early expansion of Christianity among non-Jews an important communal factor was the prevailing spiritual vacuum, itself perhaps due to the success of Rome in creating peace over a large area, the Pax Romana. Various new religions were trying to fill this vacuum. Many non-Jews were attracted to the Jewish religion in the cities of the Empire, but could not fully accept the Jewish ritual requirements which kept Jews in partial isolation from their neighbours. In the expansion of Islam within the Islamic countries a communal factor contributing to conversion was the inferior social status of the members of the protected minorities. In the nineteenth-century expansion of Christianity in Asia, Africa and elsewhere an important communal factor was the desire to share in European civilization; and this still exists to some extent. The distinction made by Muslims between their *da'wa* and Christian mission is perhaps based on the fact that they have to rely entirely on personal factors, since in western countries there is no communal factor promoting conversion to Islam.

If religions are to live together amicably, can conversion be allowed? It might perhaps be agreed that proselytizing should be abandoned, that is, activities in which the believer's main aim is not to enable others to live a fuller and more meaningful life, but to add them to his own religious group. Such activities often involve what others would regard as an unfair use of communal factors. Where only personal factors are involved, however, it would seem that there are some unusual cases where a change of religion is desirable or even essential for a person's wellbeing. Here conversion should be allowed; but such cases would be rare exceptions. In general, an individual's wellbeing is most likely to be attained if he remains within the religious culture within which he has been brought up. At this point mission is replaced by dialogue.

Dialogue may be conducted with varying degrees of formality and informality. Even one like myself who over many years has been engaged in the academic study of another religion, may be said to be involved in an inner dialogue. The essential condition of dialogue is that the participants should meet as equals, and also that, while each side should be committed to its own religion, it should feel that it may have something to receive as well as to give. The aim of dialogue is that each party should gain a better understanding of the other's religion; but experience shows that in so doing they are likely to gain deeper insights into their own beliefs.

Some Christians may feel that to engage in dialogue is to avoid the command of Christ to proclaim the gospel to every creature;[15] and some Muslims may have a corresponding feeling. Yet such feelings are basically mistaken. In dialogue one is witnessing to one's faith, and this is a way of proclaiming it. In some cases it may be a more effective way of proclaiming one's faith than the traditional methods. In effect, one is saying, "I have found something good, and I would like to share it with you". That is to say, one is bearing witness to the positive values of one's faith, but is doing so without comparing it with other faiths to their disadvantage. After witness has been borne in this way, however, it must be left to the hearers to respond to the witness in their own terms.

As the religions look towards the future in this emerging one world in which they have to live together, most of their members will be hoping that amicable forms of coexistence will be discovered. In the foreseeable future there is unlikely to be a single monolithic religion for the whole world, even if that were desirable. What one would hope is that each religion would, as the result of dialogue, achieve some understanding of the truth of other religions, and would incorporate something of this into its own vision or picture of the world. Even if it did not appreciate the assertions of other religions, it would refrain from any public declaration of their falsity, rather regarding such assertions as matters on which it was not in a position to speak.

At the heart of this emerging comity of religions, as it might be called, would be an agreement about the imprecise character of religious concepts and historical presentations, whether called mythic or iconic or by some other name, for it is this which justifies the religions in their mutual acceptance of one another. Each would accept a version of world religious history in which it had a part. Ideally the various religions would see each other as complementary and not as rivals, since each would be bearing witness to certain aspects of divine truth which were not expressed, or not so fully expressed, in the others. This would not prevent each from thinking that what it witnessed to of divine truth was more important than what the others were witnessing to. Ultimately, as was insisted on p. 133, there is no intellectual criterion of the degree of truth to be found in the different religions, but they have to be judged by the fruits in the lives of their members; and this is not something which can be settled once for all. Rather the challenge to produce worthy fruits will continue though the next and succeeding centuries, and from it there is no escape.

THE DEMANDS MADE UPON CHRISTIANS

After these general considerations about what is involved in religions living together it will be helpful to look in more detail at what is required of Christians. The essential point is that other religions have to be accepted as being on an equal footing, that is, as being just as much religions as Christianity, and as producing at least some good religious fruits. The acceptance of other religions, however, also requires the abandonment of, or at least the non-insistence on, some points of Christian belief, as found in the New Testament and the ecumenical creeds; and this is difficult for Christians, some would say impossible. The difficulty can be eased, however, by distinguishing questions of fact from questions of interpretation, since in the latter some latitude is possible.

The simplest example is that of the conception of the chosen people, that is, God's choice, first of all of Abraham, then of the Israelites, and then, as Christian theology has tended to maintain, of the Christian Church as the true inheritor of the old covenant and central to the new covenant. The concept of choice can be understood in at least two ways. It could be held that Abraham, the Israelites and the Church were chosen because they were superior to the individuals or groups around and had great merits. On the other hand, it could be held that they were chosen because of their fitness for the performance of future tasks, namely, the transmission of a special form of the knowledge of God to future generations and to the whole world eventually. This second way of understanding choice does not imply that those chosen were superior to others in any exclusivist way, and in particular it does not exclude the possibility that others, such as Muḥammad, may be chosen to perform some complementary task for God. According to this second understanding, then, the belief of Christians in these choices by God is not exclusivist.

More difficult to deal with is the assertion that Jesus is "the only-begotten (*monogenēs*) son of God" as in the Nicene creed. The term *monogenēs* comes from the apostle John,[16] and may mean no more than "only" son. A different conception is found at the beginning of the Epistle to the Hebrews,[17] where the writer says that God, who had formerly spoken to the fathers through the prophets, has now spoken to us through his son, whom he established as heir of all things, and through whom he created the worlds; a little later he adds that this son, after making a cleansing of the sins of the world, took his seat at the right hand of the majesty on high. In this conception two points are to be noted. One is that it was through the son that God created the universe; and this is reminiscent of the passage which says that it was through the Word or Logos – or perhaps we could say the divine rationality – that every thing came into being.[18] Then this aspect of God's being, his rationality or something like that, became flesh in Jesus, that is, took a human form. This appears to make Jesus unique, but it might perhaps be maintained that, in accordance with a second point, namely, his cleansing of sins, his uniqueness was derived from his unique achievement of cleansing sins.

Official Christian doctrine is that Jesus is both human and divine, and that his humanity and divinity are not intermingled; in other words, he is not a god–man or superman. Theologians and others, however, have often tended to emphasize the divinity at the expense of the humanity. Yet there is also much in the Bible which reduces the difference between Jesus and other human beings. In the account of creation it is asserted that all men and women are made in the image of God,[19] an assertion which most Muslim theologians have rejected as false. God is spoken of as a father in the Old Testament,[20] and human beings as his sons and daughters.[21] In the thought of Paul Jesus is sometimes distinguished as "the firstborn of many brethren",[22] but this is balanced elsewhere when the whole Christian community is called "the church of the firstborn (ones)".[23] Paul also distinguishes Jesus from his Christian followers by saying that, while he is truly son, they are children by adoption.[24] This again, however, can be balanced by the important passage which says that all who believe in Jesus have the right to become children of God, "those who were begotten, not of blood, not of the will of flesh, nor of the will of a male, but of God".[25]

In the light of such assertions of the divinity in some sense of all believers, it is particularly important for Christians engaging in dialogue to have a clear idea of how the sonship of Jesus differs from that of other Christians. Is it because of his unique achievement, however we describe it, or is there something else? It is to be noted at this point, too, that the uniqueness of something does not necessarily mean that it is superior to everything else, since other people also can have a unique but different task, whose uniqueness consists in its being something distinctive, not identical with any other task. I would not presume to give a solution here to these problems, but must leave it to the theologians. I would, however, like to call attention to the way in which exclusivist theological interpretations can distort translation. In the prologue to the Fourth Gospel there occur the words "we beheld his glory, *doxan hōs monogenous para patros*", where the literal translation of these Greek words would be: "a glory as of *an* only (son) from *a* (human) father"; and there is nothing contrary to Christian belief in such a translation.[26] Yet I find that the New English Bible translates: "we saw glory, such glory as befits *the* Father's only son"; and the New Jerusalem Bible has: "we saw his glory, *the* glory that he has from *the* Father as only Son of *the* Father". There is, of course, justification for such translations, but they are reading into a text what is not actually present in it. Clearly theologians and Bible translators should be more aware that we are moving into a situation of having to live together with other religions, and should realize that this places certain constraints upon them. Lest it should be thought that what has been said is intended to belittle or diminish the divinity of Jesus, I would suggest that the final result should rather be a heightening of the status of all humanity.

Apart from avoiding unjustified exclusivism, it is important that Christian theologians should work out a doctrine of the Trinity which would not remain an arcane mystery known only to a few top theologians in an intellectual stratosphere, but which would be accessible to ordinary Christians. Ordinary Christians have to meet Muslims and members of other religions and have to explain to them how, although they believe that Jesus is divine, they believe that God is one.

They may also have to meet questions about the assertion that all believers are children of God.

In a situation of dialogue I hold that the essential Christian duty is to bear witness to the historical human facts about Jesus, and then leave it to the members of other religions to form an interpretation of these facts in terms of their own tradition. The traditional Christian interpretation of these facts is in terms of late Hellenistic philosophy, which we now reject, though we have not found any generally acceptable replacement. We seem, however, to be moving into a situation in which new formulations may be accepted as alternatives to the traditional formulation, not replacing it but complementing it. Non-Christian interpretations of the teaching and achievement of Jesus, then, should not be rejected out of hand, but should be accepted at least provisionally and further discussed, until it is discovered whether Christians can accept them as alternative formulations of their own beliefs.

In dialogue with Muslims it is also important that Christians should reject the distortions of the medieval image of Islam and should develop a positive appreciation of its values. This involves accepting Muḥammad as a religious leader through whom God has worked, and that is tantamount to holding that he is in some sense a prophet. Such a view does not contradict any central Christian belief. It has, however, to be made clear to Muslims that Christians do not believe that all Muḥammad's revelations from God were infallible, even though they allow that much of divine truth was revealed to him. Arthur Arberry paid a profound tribute to the religious value of the Qur'ān in the Introduction to his translation:

> This task (of translating) was undertaken, not lightly, and carried to its conclusion at a time of great personal distress, through which it comforted and sustained the writer in a manner for which he will always be grateful. He therefore acknowledges his gratitude to whatever power or Power inspired the man and the Prophet who first recited these scriptures.[27]

To this personal statement may be added an official one from the section on Islam in the Declaration on the Relation of the Church to non-Christian Religions issued by the Second Vatican Council in 1965:[28]

> The Church also regards with esteem the Muslims who worship the one, subsistent, merciful and almighty God, the Creator of heaven

and earth, who has spoken to man. Islam willingly traces its descent back to Abraham, and just as he submitted himself to God, the Muslims endeavour to submit themselves to his mysterious decrees. They venerate Jesus as a prophet, without, however, recognizing him as God, and they pay honour to his virgin mother Mary and sometimes also invoke her with devotion. Further, they expect a day of judgement when God will raise all men from the dead and reward them. For this reason they attach importance to the moral life and worship God, mainly by prayer, alms-giving and fasting. If in the course of the centuries there has arisen not infrequent dissension and hostility between Christian and Muslim, this sacred Council now urges everyone to forget the past, to make sincere efforts at mutual understanding and to work together in protecting and promoting for the benefit of all men, social justice, good morals as well as peace and freedom.

THE DEMANDS MADE UPON MUSLIMS

For Muslims also, if they are to live alongside other religions, it will be necessary to abandon their exclusivism. This means admitting that, even if Islam has all the truth required by the whole human race to the end of time, there may be complementary ways of expressing this truth. It would also appear that Muslims would have to reinterpret their conception of the finality of Islam and of Muḥammad's being the last prophet. This last point presupposes that there has been a series of pure and perfect revelations from God, but this is not borne out by what we now know of the history of religion. It would seem that Muslims would have to admit that religions like Hinduism and Buddhism also received something from God, though not in a form resembling that of the revelation to Muḥammad.

In respect of Muslim–Christian relations it is essential that Muslims accept the historicity of the Bible and reject the doctrine of its corruption. That doctrine contradicts known facts, such as the existence of manuscripts dating from long before the time of Muḥammad. Throughout this century and last the Bible has been the object of searching literary criticism by Christians and nominal Christians. Some of this criticism has been very radical, and there have been conservative Christians who accepted little of it. Most Christians who understand the literary critics, however, would accept the main points. This means admitting that some of the books of the Bible have had a complex history of being compiled and edited, but it would be vigorously maintained that such processes were subject to the inspiration of the Holy Spirit, and do not detract from the religious value of the Bible. What Muslims are being asked to accept, then, is that the Old and New Testaments in our hands are identical with the scriptures which have been inspiring Jews and Christians from the earliest times.

There are special problems with regard to the New Testament. Literary criticism has shown that the gospels present the life and teaching of Jesus as it was understood by Christians a generation or so after the events, but a large body of Christian scholars hold that there is nevertheless a core of genuine historical material. What Muslims and other non-Christians are asked to accept in this world where religions mix is this core of historical fact about the teaching and achievement of Jesus as a human being, but without the theological interpretations. If the historical human facts are accepted, it is then up to each religion to interpret these in accordance with its own tradition. In his articles entitled "Towards an Islamic Christology" Mahmoud Ayoub has begun to do this for Muslims.[29]

Some Christians probably feel that it would have been preferable to have a more directly transmitted and so more accurate record of the teaching of Jesus (and may also feel similarly about the Old Testament). It would be better, however, to be thankful for all that it has been given to us to know about Jesus, and to accept the fact that this is how God has willed that these truths should come to us. This implies that God chooses to work through imperfect human instruments. Doubtless a prophet or religious leader has to have many good qualities, but he does not need to be perfect in all respects; and the same holds of the transmitters of religious truth. God's use of imperfect human instruments appears to be one of the objective historical facts which many Muslims are unwilling to accept.

TOWARDS A COMITY OF RELIGIONS

There are grounds for thinking that a single world religion, if it were monolithic, would be undesirable, so that our aim for the most distant foreseeable future should be what has been described above as a comity of religions. The last word may be given to a Muslim who envisages something like this:[30]

> Islam may be able to help humanity in its quest for a way out of its predicament of destruction and alienation, but only when Muslims

live equally seriously the piety of their faith and its social, political, ethical and economic demands. In the end, the challenge of Islam as an institutionalized religion is the inner Islam, or surrender of all things to God. It is the courage to let God be God in our individual lives, society and world affairs. This is a challenge not for Muslims alone, but for all the people of God. If domestic politics and foreign policy in the West could be truly Christianized and the world of Islam in all its aspects Islamized, then ''Dār al-Islām'' could include the Church, and the Church would see the entire world as the ''mystical body of Christ''. Then will the righteous servant of God and the meek ''inherit the earth''.

Notes

Abbreviations

N. 3/16, etc. – chapter 3, note 16.
EI[1], *EI*[2] – *Encyclopaedia of Islam* (Leiden and London, first edition, 1913–34; second edition, 1954).

Note

Roman numerals denote volume numbers.

1 The Christianity encountered by Islam

1 Acts 14:11.
2 I have not attempted to give detailed references for the statements in this and the following sections. They are much abbreviated summaries of work I did over forty years ago in Jerusalem, using such books as were available in the libraries of St George's Cathedral and the Ecole Biblique. Up-to-date references will be found in the *Encyclopedia of Religion*, Mircea Eliade (ed.) (New York: Macmillan, 1987) in articles on individual theologians and in general articles such as: Creeds, Christian; Dogma.
3 Philippians 2:7,8.
4 Hans Küng *et al.*, *Christianity and the World Religions: Paths to Dialogue with Islam, Hinduism and Buddhism* (London: Collins, 1986).
5 Full details in J. Spencer Trimingham, *Christianity among the Arabs in Pre-Islamic Times* (London: Longman, 1979).
6 Georg Graf, *Geschichte der christlichen arabischen Literatur*, vol. 1 (Vatican City, 1944).
7 Ibn-Hishām, *Sīra*, F. Wüstenfeld (ed.) (Göttingen: Dieterich, 1858–60), p. 153. Ibn-Hishām (d.*c.*833) edited the main part of the *Sīra* or Life of Muḥammad by Ibn-Isḥāq (d.767), with some additional notes and some omissions. Alfred Guillaume in his English translation, *The Life of Muhammad* (London: Oxford University Press, 1955) adds from other sources some of the paragraphs Ibn-Hishām omitted, and places his additions at the end. See also p. 38 this volume and note 3/20.
8 Ibn-Hishām, *Sīra*, F. Wüstenfeld (ed.) (Göttingen: Dieterich, 1858–60),

p. 144; see also Watt, *Muhammad at Mecca* (Oxford: Clarendon Press, 1953), p. 15; the man's mother was an Abyssinian – Ibn-Ḥabīb, *Muḥabbar* I. Lichtenstadter (ed.) (Hyderabad: 1942), p. 307.

2 The Qur'ānic perception of Christianity

1 3:137; 6:6, 11; 17:17; 30:9; etc.
2 Full lists will be found in Watt, *Bell's Introduction to the Qur'ān* (Edinburgh: Edinburgh University Press, 1970), p. 132.
3 2:87; cf. 5:44.
4 29:27; cf. 57:26.
5 2:78–80; 34:10; and cf. Psalm 148:10f.
6 3:67; etc. For *ḥanīf* see p. 16 this volume.
7 Cf. Watt, *Muhammad at Mecca* (Oxford: Clarendon Press, 1953), p. 51; also Watt, *Muhammad's Mecca* (Edinburgh: Edinburgh University Press, 1988, p. 59).
8 2:140; cf. 3:67, quoted on p. 14 this volume.
9 *Muhammad's Mecca*, p. 37f.
10 Watt, art. Ḥanīf in *EI*², slightly updating the treatment in *Muhammad at Mecca*, pp. 162–4.
11 Geoffrey Parrinder, *Jesus in the Qur'ān* (London: Faber, 1965), p. 70.
12 Parrinder, op. cit., p. 83f.
13 Ibid, pp. 105–21.
14 See pp. 126–9 this volume.
15 Parrinder, op. cit., pp. 126–41.
16 2:40, 89, 91; etc.
17 See p. 72 this volume and note 5/27.
18 See *Muhammad at Mecca*, p. 53.
19 See *Muhammad's Mecca*, p. 67.
20 Matthew 7:16, 20.
21 See Thomas Merton, *A Vow of Conversation* (Basingstoke: Lamp Press, 1988), p. 100.

3 The elaboration of Qur'ānic perceptions

1 This was discussed in my article "The early development of the Muslim attitude to the Bible", *Early Islam* (Edinburgh: Edinburgh University Press, 1991), pp. 77–85.
2 See the notes on verse 5:41 in Sale's translation (various editions).
3 See Rudi Paret, *Der Koran: Kommentar und Konkordanz* (Stuttgart: Kohlhammer, 1971), on Sura 6:21.
4 Aṭ-Ṭabarī, *Tafsīr* (Cairo, 1904) i, p. 278 (on 2:75) and v, 70f. (on 4:46).
5 A. Mingana, *Woodbrooke Studies* (Cambridge: Heffer, 1928), ii, 35f.
6 See pp. 65–7f. this volume; also I. Goldziher, "Über muhammedanische Polemik gegen Ahl al-Kitāb" in *Gesammelte Schriften* (Hildesheim: Olms, 1968), ii, 1–47, esp. pp. 24–32.
7 2:42, 77, 140, 146, 159, 174; 3:71; 5:15; 6:91.
8 John 14:16, 26; 15:26; 16:7.

9 See p. 63 this volume.
10 Watt, "His Name is Ahmad", *Moslem World*, xliii (1953), 110f. and *Early Islam*, see note 3/1.
11 Ibn-Hishām, *Sīra*, F. Wüstenfeld (ed.) (Göttingen: Dieterich, 1858–60), p. 149f.
12 See A. Guthrie and E.F.F. Bishop, "The Paraclete, Al-Munhamanna and Aḥmad", *Moslem World*, xli (1951), pp. 251–6; A. Guillaume, in *Al-Andalus*, xv (1950), pp. 289–96, and note to his translation of the *Sīra*, p. 104.
13 Ibn-Sa'd, *Ṭabaqāt*, (ed.) E. Sachau, 9 vols, (Leiden: Brill, 1905, etc.).
14 Watt, "The early development of the Muslim attitude to the Bible" (see note 3/1), §2.
15 Ibn-Hishām, pp. 115–17; translated in Watt, *Muhammad at Mecca*, pp. 36–8.
16 'Alī ibn-Rabbān aṭ-Ṭabarī, *Kitāb ad-dīn wa-d-dawla*, (ed.) A. Mingana (Manchester: 1922).
17 See EI^2, art. Ḳāṣṣ (C. Pellat).
18 EI^2, art. Ka'b al-Aḥbār; Fuat Sezgin, *Geschichte des arabischen Schrifttums* (Leiden: Brill, 1967), i. p. 304f.
19 Sezgin, op. cit., i., pp. 305–7; Yāqūt, *Irshād* (Dictionary of Learned Men) (ed.) D.S. Margoliouth, 7 vols, London, E.J.W. Gibb Memorial Series, 1923–6, vii, p. 232.
20 Columbia, SC: University of South Carolina Press.
21 Ibn-Hishām, p. 972.
22 Guillaume, pp. 651–8, translating aṭ-Ṭabarī, i, 1561–9; see note 1/7.
23 Watt, *The Faith and Practice of al-Ghazālī* (London: Allen and Unwin, 1953), p. 44f.
24 Watt, *The Formative Period of Islamic Thought* (Edinburgh: Edinburgh University Press, 1973), p. 2.
25 J. Waardenburg, "World religions as seen in the light of Islam" in A.T. Welch and P. Cachia (eds) *Islam: Past Influence and Present Challenge* (Edinburgh: Edinburgh University Press, 1979), pp. 276–95.
26 Watt, *Islamic Fundamentalism and Modernity* (London: Routledge, 1988), p. 13.
27 The quotations are from Ibn-'Abd-al-Barr (d.1070), *Jāmi' Bayān al-'ilm*, and are translated in W.M. Watt, "The early development . . ." (see n.3/1), p. 84.
28 EI^2, art. Isrā'īliyyāt (G. Vajda); I. Goldziher, "Isrā'īliyyāt" in *Gesammelte Schriften* (Hildesheim: Olms, 1970), iv, 323–6.
29 G.H.A. Juynboll, *The Authenticity of the Tradition Literature: Discussions in Modern Egypt* (Leiden: Brill, 1969), p. 121.
30 Juynboll, op. cit., p. 137.
31 Aṭ-Ṭabarī, *Akhbār ar-rusul wa-l-mulūk* (Annales) (ed.) de Goeje *et al.*, 13 vols (Leiden: Brill), i, p. 1897f.; the whole is now being translated into English as *The History of al-Ṭabarī* under the editorship of Ehsan Yar-Shater (Albany, NY: State University of New York Press, 1987, continuing).
32 Aṭ-Ṭabarī, *Annales*, i, p. 740f.
33 *Murūj adh-dhahab*, text and French translation by C. Barbier de Meynard and Pavet de Courteille, 7 vols (Paris: Société Asiatique, 1861–76).

34 *Murūj* i, p. 122. For the incident see Luke 4:16–21; for the quotation see Isaiah 42:1 and Matthew 12:18; but cf. Psalms 2:7. The following quotation is from *Murūj* i, p. 124.
35 *EI*², art. Ibn al-Athīr (2).
36 H.A.R. Gibb, *Modern Trends in Islam* (Chicago: University of Chicago Press, 1947), p. 125.
37 *Murūj* iv, pp. 107–9.
38 Ibn-al-Athīr, *Kāmil* (Cairo: 1348 AH (AD 1929), i, p. 172.

4 The encounter with Greek philosophy

1 Moritz Steinschneider, *Die arabischen Übersetzungen aus dem Griechischen* (Graz: Akademische Verlagsanstalt, 1960, reprint).
2 See my *Formative Period* (n.3/24), pp. 186–95.
3 *Formative Period*, pp. 303–12.
4 Ibid, 206–8.
5 *The Spiritual Physick*, tr. A.J. Arberry (London: Murray, 1950).
6 *Tahāfut al-falāsifa* (ed.) M. Bouyges (Beirut: Imprimesie Catholique, 1927).
7 Watt, *Faith and Practice* (n.3/23), p. 37f. For al-Ghazālī in general see Watt, *Muslim Intellectual* (Edinburgh: Edinburgh University Press, 1963).
8 *EI*², arts (al-)Īdjī (J. van Ess): (al-)Djurdjānī (A.S. Tritton).
9 *EI*², art. Fakhr al-Dīn al-Rāzī (G.C. Anawati).
10 Louis Gardet and M.M. Anawati, *Introduction à la théologie musulmane* (Paris: Vrin, 1948).
11 *Averroes' Tahāfut al-Tahāfut*, trans. Simon van den Bergh, two vols (London: Luzac, 1954).
12 Moritz Steinschneider, *Die europäische Übersetzungen aus dem Arabischen bis Mitte des 17. Jahrhunderts* (Graz: Akademische Verlagsanstalt, 1956); Eugene A. Myers, *Arabic Thought and the Western World* (New York: Ungar, 1964).
13 Gibb, *Modern Trends* (n.3/36), pp. 18–20.
14 Gardet and Anawati, op. cit., pp. 76–8.
15 Cf. J.A. Weisheipl, art. Scholasticism, in *Encyclopedia of Religion* (see n.1/2).
16 G.C. Anawati, in *Cambridge History of Islam*, P.M. Holt, A.K.S. Lambton, and B. Lewis (eds) (Cambridge: Cambridge University Press, 1970), ii, p. 778.

5 Encounters under Muslim rule

1 Watt, *Muhammad at Medina* (Oxford: Clarendon Press, 1956), p. 145f.
2 T.W. Arnold, *The Preaching of Islam: A History of the Propagation of the Muslim Faith*, 3rd edn (London: Luzac, 1935), pp. 121–30.
3 Ibn-Hishām, *Sīra*, F. Wüstenfeld (ed.) (Göttingen: Dieterich, 1858–60), p. 403.
4 *Woodbrooke Studies* (see n.3/5), ii, pp. 1–162. Cf. Robert Caspar, "Les Versions arabes du dialogue entre le Catholicos Timothée et le calife al-Mahdī", *Islamochristiana*, iii (1977), pp. 107–75.
5 London: SPCK, 2nd edn, 1885; discussed at length by G. Graf, op. cit.

(see n.1/6), ii, pp. 135–45; also Sezgin, op. cit. (n.3/18), i, pp. 612f.; Arnold, *Preaching of Islam*, pp. 84f., 428–35 (an abbreviated translation of the Muslim's letter).

6 For bibliographical information see: Moritz Steinschneider, *Polemische und apologetische Literatur in arabischer Sprache* (Leipzig: 1877, repr. Hildesheim: Olms, 1966); "Bibliographie du dialogue islamo-chrétien" in *Islamochristiana*, i (1975), pp. 125–76; ii (1976), pp. 187–249; continued in later vols. An initial study was: Erdmann Fritsch, *Islam und Christentum im Mittelalter: Beiträge zur Geschichte der muslimischen Polemik gegen das Christentum in arabischer Sprache* (Breslau: Müller u. Seifert, 1930). There is a useful recent survey by Waardenburg, op. cit. (see n.3/25), esp. pp. 258–69.

7 *EI*[2], art. (al-)Djāḥiẓ (C. Pellat).

8 See n.3/16.

9 *Kitāb at-Tamhīd*, (ed.) R.J. McCarthy (Beirut: Librairie Orientale, 1957), pp. 75–103.

10 *Kitāb al-Irshād*, ed. and tr. J.D. Luciani (Paris: Leroux, 1938), pp. 28–30 (on substance and hypostasis).

11 *EI*[2], art. Ibn Ḥazm (R. Arnaldez). References are to a Baghdad edn (n.d., ?1960) in five vols.

12 1 Corinthians 1:24: Christ the power of God and the wisdom of God.

13 *Ar-Radd al-jamīl li ilāhiyyat ʿĪsā bi-ṣarīḥ al-injīl* ("Refutation excellente de la divinité de Jésus Christ d'après les évangiles"), ed. and tr. Robert Chidiac, Paris, 1939. It had previously been discussed by Louis Massignon in "Le Christ dans les évangiles selon al-Ghazālī", *Revue des études islamiques*, iv, (1932), pp. 491–536, reprinted in his *Opera Minora* (Beirut: Dar al-Maaref, 1963), ii, pp. 523–36.

14 There is a long convincing critique of its authenticity by Hava Lazarus-Yafeh in her *Studies in al-Ghazzali* (Jerusalem: Magnes Press, 1975), pp. 458–87.

15 *Al-Qisṭās al-mustaqīm* ("The Just Balance") in a collection *Al-Jawāhir al-ghawālī* (Cairo: AH 1353/AD 1934), 156–203, esp. p. 175f. Massignon, *Opera Minora*, ii, p. 524.

16 *Al-Maqṣad al-asnā* (Cairo 1324 AH), pp. 73–5; cf. Massignon, op. cit., pp. 533f.

17 *Nihāyat al-iqdām fī ʿilm al-kalām*, ed. and tr. A. Guillaume (London: Oxford University Press, 1934).

18 W. Cureton (ed.) (London: Madden, 1842): Sh. Aḥmad Fahmy Muḥammad (ed.) (Cairo, 1948) in three vols; German translation by Theodor Haarbrücker (Halle: 1850–1). The section on Christianity is found on pp. 171–9 (London) and ii, pp. 32–52 (Cairo).

19 See my translation "Ash-Shahrastānī's account of Christian Doctrine" in *Islamochristiana*, ix (1983), pp. 249–59; references are to the paging there. The translation also appeared in *Hamdard Islamicus* (Karachi), vi (1983), pp. 57–68 with slightly different comments.

20 *EI*[1], art. Murtadd (W. Heffening).

21 Migne, *Patrologia Graeca*, vol. 94, col. 764ff.; the two versions of the Disceptatio are in Migne, vols 94, col. 1585ff. and 96, col. 1335–48.

22 Vol. 2 of Georg Graf's *Geschichte der christlichen arabischen Literatur* (Vatican City, 1947), devotes over 500 pages to Christians writing in Arabic up to the middle of the fifteenth century.

23 4.171; 3.45 (p. 19 this volume): see also Parrinder, op. cit. (see n.2/11), pp. 45–51.
24 Apparently from the Psalm; but it is doubtful if 33:6 is intended, though it was quoted by Timothy.
25 Timothy in *Woodbrooke Studies* (see n.3/5), ii, pp. 22, 69, etc.
26 Cf. p. 65 this volume.
27 Timothy, op. cit., pp. 61f., 54, 36.
28 See p. 64 this volume and n.5/5.

6 Encounters with medieval Europe

1 A detailed presentation of the matters in this section will be found in my book, *Islamic Spain* (Edinburgh: Edinburgh University Press, 1965).
2 Quoted from *Islamic Spain*, p. 170.
3 A fuller study of this topic will be found in my article "Perceptions of the Crusades" in the Bausani memorial volume to be published in Italy.
4 *A Study of History* (London: Oxford University Press, 1934–54), v, p. 242.
5 *Oxford English Dictionary*, s.v.
6 Edward Gibbon, *Decline and Fall of the Roman Empire*, various editions, Ch. 58.
7 Steven Runciman, *A History of the Crusades* (Harmondsworth: Penguin, 1965), iii, pp. 480.
8 *Polémique Byzantine contre l'Islam (VIIIe–XIIIe S.)* (Leiden: Brill, 1972), esp. pp. 359–65. See also Alain Ducellier, *Le miroir de l'Islam: Musulmans et chrétiens d'Orient au Moyen Age* (Paris: 1971).
9 Norman Daniel, *Islam and the West: the Making of an Image* (Edinburgh: Edinburgh University Press, 1960), pp. 7, 12. The rest of this section relies heavily on this work.
10 James Kritzeck, *Peter the Venerable and Islam* (Princeton: Princeton University Press, 1964), p. 23.
11 For details see Kritzeck, op. cit. In older works he is mistakenly called Retenensis.
12 See Daniel, op. cit., Bibliography A.
13 James Waltz, "Muḥammad and the Muslims in St. Thomas Aquinas" in *Muslim World*, lxvi (1976): 81–95. This makes important additions to the treatment of Aquinas in Daniel, op. cit.
14 For what follows see my book, *The Influence of Islam on Medieval Europe* (Edinburgh: Edinburgh University Press, 1972), pp. 72–80.
15 Waltz, op. cit., quoting *Summa Theologica*, II.1, q. 10, art. 8.
16 Daniel, op. cit., p. 242.
17 Edward W. Said, *Orientalism* (New York: Vintage Books, 1979), p. 3.

7 The background of the modern encounter

1 Kritzeck, *Peter the Venerable*, p. viif. (See n.6/10.)
2 See note 6/17.
3 Thomas Merton, *Love and Living* (New York: Bantam Books, 1980), pp. 70–82; the quotation is from 77f.
4 Watt, *Influence* (n.6/14), p. 80; another example is John of Segovia, cf. R.W. Southern, *Western Views of Islam in the Middle Ages* (Cambridge: Mass., Harvard University Press, 1962), p. 88.

5 B. Lewis, *The Emergence of Modern Turkey* (London: Oxford University Press, 1961), p. 124.

8 The modern encounter

1 *Orientalism*, p. 241. (See n.6/17.)
2 Lewis, *Emergence*, pp. 48f., 58f., 82, 122–5. (See n.7/5).
3 Akbar S. Ahmed, *Discovering Islam* (London: Routledge, 1988); see also W. Cantwell Smith, *Modern Islam in India*, 2nd edn (London: Gollancz, 1947).
4 *The Spirit of Islam*, 3rd edn (London: Christophers, 1922); the first edition was entitled *A Critical Examination of the Life and Teachings of Mohammed* (London: 1873).
5 See art. Mission – Christian (Stephen Neill) in *Encyclopedia of Religion* (see n.1/2). In an article on "Roots of Muslim–Christian conflict" Professor M. Ayoub describes attacks on Christian missions by Egyptian writers (*Muslim World*, lxxix (1989): 25–45). See also remarks by Isma'il Faruqi reported in *Islamochristiana*, ii (1976): 147.
6 W. Muir, *The Mohammedan Controversy, etc.* (Edinburgh: Clark, 1897), esp. pp. 40–2, 86–9.
7 Tr. by R.H. Weakley (London: CMS, 1867); it had been published in Persian in 1835 and in Urdu in 1843.
8 Constance E. Padwick, *Temple Gairdner of Cairo* (London: SPCK, 1929).
9 Abdallah Laroui, *The Crisis of the Arab Intellectual: Traditionalism or Historicism?* tr. by Diarmid Cammell (Berkeley: University of California Press, 1976), p. 44.
10 Ibid, p. 80.
11 Published as a book; see n.3/36.
12 See n.6/17.
13 Ibid, pp. 37–9.
14 Ibid, p. 300.
15 Quoted from John Hick and Brian Hebblethwaite (eds), *Christianity and other Religions: Selected Readings* (London: Collins, 1980), p. 98.
16 *Orientalism*, p. 163. (See n.6/17.)
17 Leila Ahmed, *Edward W. Lane* (London: Longman, 1978), p. 38f.
18 *Orientalism*, p. 280. (See n.6/17).
19 George Makdisi, *The Rise of Colleges* (Edinburgh: Edinburgh University Press, 1981), esp. pp. 21–32, 153–9.
20 *Orientalism*, p. 272. (See n.6/17.)
21 Gustav Pfannmüller, *Handbuch der Islam-Literatur* (Berlin: de Gruyter, 1923), pp. 60, 63f.; Daniel, *Islam and the West* (see n.6/9), p. 295; G. Endress, *An Introduction to Islam*, tr. Carole Hillenbrand (Edinburgh: Edinburgh University Press, 1988), p. 11. A critical survey of orientalism relevant to points discussed here is: Maxime Rodinson "The western image and western studies of Islam", in J. Schacht and C.E. Bosworth (eds), *The Legacy of Islam*, 2nd edn (Oxford: Clarendon Press, 1974), pp. 9–62.
22 Many editions, and still in print. The revised edition by E.M. Wherry (Boston: Houghton Mifflin, 1882), is best avoided because of the hostile attitude towards Islam in the additional notes.

23 (London: Smith Elder, 1894). For earlier articles by him see n.8/6.
24 Op. cit., p. 500f.
25 Mohammed Arkoun, *Ouvertures sur l'Islam* (Paris: Grancher, 1989), p. 120; see also p. 119 this volume.
26 See Watt, *Muhammad's Mecca* (n.2/7), pp. 51–3 with further references.
27 *Muhammedanische Studien*, vol. 2 (Halle: 1890): Eng. tr. by S.M. Stern and C.R. Butler (London: Allen and Unwin, 1971).
28 (Oxford: Clarendon Press, 1950.)
29 Sezgin, op. cit. (n.3/18), i, 53–84.
30 Emad Eldin Shahir, "Muḥammad Rashīd Riḍa's Perspectives on the West as reflected in Al-Manār", *Muslim World*, lxxix (1989), 116.
31 The examples are taken from a pamphlet by Syed Athar Husain, *The Quran and the Orientalists* (Lucknow: 1982).
32 Laura and Lonsdale Ragg, *The Gospel of Barnabas* (Oxford: Clarendon Press, 1907).
33 *Évangile de Barnabé*, Luigi Cirillo and Michel Frémaux (Paris: Beauchesne, 1977), 598pp.
34 Jan Slomp, "The Gospel in dispute", *Islamochristiana*, iv (1978), pp. 67–112.
35 John Hick (ed.) (London: SCM, 1977). See also: *Incarnation and Myth: the Debate Continued*, Michael Goulder (ed.) (London: SCM, 1979).
36 (Jeddah, 1978); the first quotation is from p. 14.
37 Op cit., p. 47.
38 *Ouvertures sur l'Islam* (n.8/25), p. 120.
39 *Islamic Fundamentalism and Modernity*, pp. 1–23 (see n.3/26).
40 Romans 13:1.
41 P. 93, this volume and note 7/3.
42 Ibid, p. 78.
43 Ibid, p. 77.
44 Ibid, p. 82.
45 *Islamochristiana*, xiii (1987), 133f., 141–54.
46 Ibid, vii (1981), 283–8.
47 Ibid, xii (1986), 135–61, esp. 161.
48 Ibid, v (1979), 1–5; viii (1982), 1–7.
49 Ibid, v (1979), 126, in an article by Christian Troll on "Christian–Muslim relations in India: a critical survey", 119–45.
50 Kenneth Cragg, *Counsels in Contemporary Islam* (Edinburgh: Edinburgh University Press, 1965), p. 108; *City of Wrong: a Friday in Jerusalem* (London: Bles, 1959).
51 *Islamochristiana* vi (1980), 101–3; xiv (1988). 17–49.
52 The Hague: Mouton, 1980.
53 *Muslim World*, lxvi (1976), 163–88; lxx (1980), 91–121.
54 "Muslim Views on Christianity: some modern examples", *Islamochristiana*, x (1984), 49–70; "A Muslim appreciation of Christian holiness", ibid, xi (1985), 91–8; "Roots of Muslim–Christian conflict", n.8/5.
55 (Edinburgh: Edinburgh University Press, 1981).
56 (London: SCM, 1989).
57 *Knowledge and the Sacred* (Edinburgh: Edinburgh University Press, 1982), p. 110.

9 Towards the future

1 See esp. pp. 293–302 (see n.6/17).
2 P. 42 this volume and note 3/26.
3 Cf. Watt, *Islam and Christianity Today* (London: Routledge, 1983), p. 119; *Islamic Fundamentalism*, p. 81f. (see n.3/26).
4 *Islamic Fundamentalism*, p. 78f.
5 Merton, op. cit. (n.7/3), p. 73.
6 *Ouvertures* (n.8/25), p. 88; cf. p. 121.
7 P. 25 this volume.
8 "Whatever path men choose is mine" in Hick and Hebblethwaite (eds), *Christianity and other Religions* (n.8/15), pp. 171–90, esp. 174–7.
9 Matthew 7:15–20.
10 Genesis 9:8–17.
11 Malachi 1:11.
12 Matthew 8:11f.
13 Sura 4:122f.
14 Vincent Donovan, *Christianity Rediscovered* (London: SCM, 1982), p. 66.
15 Mark 16:15; Matthew 28:19.
16 John 1:14, 18; 3:16, 18; 1 John 4:9.
17 Hebrews 1:1–4.
18 John 1:3.
19 Genesis 1:26f.; 5:1f.
20 2 Samuel 7:14; 1 Chronicles 17:13; Psalm 89:26; Jeremiah 3:19; 31:9.
21 Isaiah 43:6; quoted in 2 Corinthians 6:18.
22 Romans 8:26.
23 Hebrews 12:23.
24 Romans 8:14–17; Galatians 4:4–7; Ephesians 1:5.
25 John 1:13.
26 John 1:14.
27 Arthur J. Arberry, *The Koran Interpreted* (London: Oxford University Press, 1964), p. xiif.
28 Quoted from Hick and Hebblethwaite (eds), op. cit. (n.8/15), p. 82f.
29 See pp. 126–9 this volume.
30 Mahmoud Ayoub, op. cit. (n.8/5), last paragraph; for the last phrase he has a reference to Sura 21:105 and Matthew 5:5.

Index

Note

The Arabic article al-, ash-, etc. is neglected in the alphabetical arrangement.